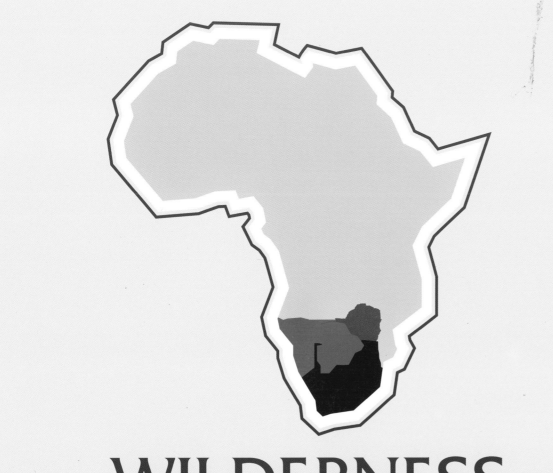

WILDERNESS HERITAGE

Colin Mead

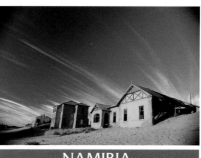

ISBN 0-620-19401-4

Published privately by:

COLIN MEAD
P.O. Box 68914
Bryanston
2021
South Africa

Telephone (011) 706-4425
         (011) 706-5360
         082 456 2984

Graphic Design by CENTURA CREATIVE SERVICES
Repro by THE BUREAU
Printed by HORTORS PRINT (PTY) LIMITED

Southern Africa fascinates everyone lucky enough to experience her, but very few of us can explain why.

Still fewer can convey the sensation of that mysterious attraction to others.

In this book Colin Mead will succeed in doing this for a host of readers. Driven by his own overpowering interest, he has ranged all over the sub-continent. Equipped to the best professional standards as a photographer, he has captured, again and again, the definitive images of his own experience. These are here laid out in a format which encourages us to follow in his footsteps, but which also permits us the vicarious enjoyment of an armchair expedition. Doing either will open our eyes to new insights and sensations; it will also make us acquainted with the multi-faceted personality of the author.

Both are rewarding — enjoy the trip!

Derek Keys

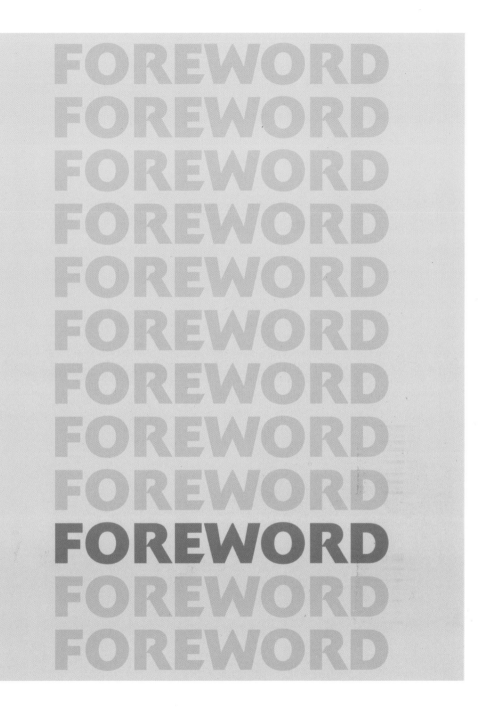

DEDICATION

*To my wife Margaret, to Tracy and Noel,
Darryl and Hayley, and future grandchildren.*

This is primarily a portfolio of photographs … one man's testament to a few of the wild places of Southern Africa. However, I believe that non-photographers will find much to interest them, too, because this book is dedicated to every person who cares about the preservation of the raw beauty and fragile balance of nature, not only in Southern Africa — but in all the world.

Wilderness Heritage has, to some extent, been conceived as a coffee-table book, with the emphasis on photography. But I thought it might be useful to include a text section as well, to provide practical information for anyone who would like to visit some of the areas covered in this book. I have tried to pack as much useful, practical information into it as the limited space will allow.

I realise, of course, that many other authors and photographers have dealt in great depth with each of the natural sanctuaries that form the subject matter of this volume. I am all too aware that I have hardly scratched the surface, and that one could live many lifetimes without having the time to do full justice to the splendour of even one small part of untamed Africa. But I hope that the following pages will give you an inkling of what to expect, and — more importantly — the motivation to visit these places for yourself. Every one of the images in this book could have been taken by you, from your vehicle, without leaving the road. I have enjoyed no special access privileges in any of the National Parks or areas that I photographed.

If you are interested in the technical side of things, here is some information about the camera equipment that I used for the photographs in this book. The majority were taken with a Canon T-90 body and a choice of three Canon zoom lenses — a 28–85 mm lens, a 100–300 mm lens, and a 150–600 mm telephoto (which was used for most of the wildlife pictures). My favourite film is Fuji Velvia, a colour-slide film (ISO 50) with good colour saturation. Velvia is classed as a "slow" film, which means that there can be problems when shooting in low light, with a telephoto lens, or when longish time exposures are required. But I use it to achieve the fine grain necessary for high-quality colour reproduction. (When I'm not actually taking photographs, I spend a considerable amount of time in the darkroom making enlargements of my pictures. If you would like to enquire about original prints of any photographs in this book — or others from my picture files — please feel free to contact me).

INTRODUCTION

This introduction would not be complete without thanks to my wife, Margaret, for her infinite patience, and all the work she has done for me on this book. And to Jules Cohen, a big "thank you" for his creative layout and typography — as well as for being brave (foolhardy?) enough to help with all the books that I have previously published. Last, but perhaps most importantly, I would like to thank ABSA Bank for their faith in me and their financial support. It has been a real pleasure working with all of you!

There's a good reason why this book is called *Wilderness Heritage*. "Heritage" is defined in the dictionary* as "…evidence of the past, such as…the unspoilt natural environment, considered collectively as the inheritance of present-day society". You and I and all mankind are curators, entrusted with the safekeeping of our environment. Virtually every place referred to in this book is under threat from one man-related source or another, an ugly indictment of humanity's cavalier disregard for almost every other species on Earth. The rate of destruction of the natural environment is horrifying. We must strive at all times to conserve and enjoy our inheritance, not to destroy it. We all have a responsibility to preserve this planet for our children, and their children, and for every generation after that. It is the only habitat we have. Extinction, I need hardly remind you, is forever. If this book helps just one person to achieve a greater awareness and appreciation of the beauty of our wildlife and scenic heritage, as well as a respect for the delicate ecosystems, then I will have succeeded to some small degree in achieving what I set out to do.

Let us all work to make this world a better place … today … tomorrow … forever … for everyone.

Colin Mead

---

* *Collins English Dictionary, Second Edition*

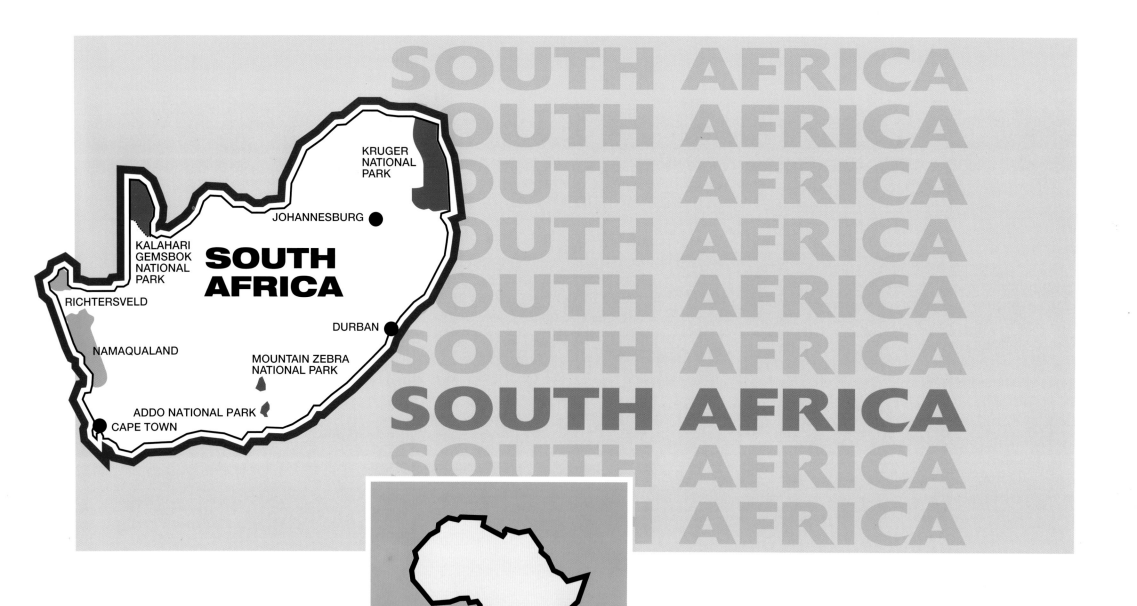

KRUGER NATIONAL PARK

JOHANNESBURG

KALAHARI GEMSBOK NATIONAL PARK

SOUTH AFRICA

RICHTERSVELD

DURBAN

NAMAQUALAND

MOUNTAIN ZEBRA NATIONAL PARK

ADDO NATIONAL PARK

CAPE TOWN

SOUTH AFRICA
SOUTH AFRICA
SOUTH AFRICA
SOUTH AFRICA
SOUTH AFRICA
SOUTH AFRICA
SOUTH AFRICA
SOUTH AFRICA
SOUTH AFRICA
SOUTH AFRICA

KALAHARI GEMSBOK NATIONAL PARK

This National Park is sandwiched between Namibia in the west and Botswana in the east, and lies due north of Upington. It's a long way from anywhere — which is the secret of its unique charm.

The region is arid and semi-desert, bordering on the Gemsbok National Park in Botswana. There are no fences separating the two parks, which is a rather neat arrangement because it means that the animals can migrate freely between them.

If you're a collector of trivia, you'll be interested to learn that the Kalahari Gemsbok park was proclaimed in 1931 to help counter the poaching menace, and is closely associated with the family name of Le Riche. The first ranger, Johannes Le Riche, died of malaria after the great flood of 1934.

There are three camps, offering accommodation and camping spots. The largest of these is at Twee Rivieren in the south, which is the only access point to the park. It lies close to the point where the two main rivers come together (hence the name, which obviously means "Two Rivers", even if you don't speak Dutch). The second largest camp is Nossob, on the western bank of the river of that name, on the Botswana border. From Twee Rivieren it takes about 4 hours to reach Nossob. The third, and smallest camp is Mata Mata, on the Auob River in the west, bordering Namibia. You'll find it by driving about 2 1/2 hours northwest of Twee Rivieren. Petrol and a fairly basic selection of groceries are available at all three camps, while Twee Rivieren boasts the additional amenity of a swimming pool.

The Nossob River last flowed in 1963 and the river beds are usually dry, allowing the two major roads to follow their course. Another pair of roads go across the dunes (rather like a dusty roller-coaster ride) and link the river bed roads. Generally speaking, the roads are in good condition, and a 4-wheel drive vehicle is not necessary. If your car breaks down for any reason, don't wander away from it. Each evening the camp authorities check all the returning vehicles and go out to search for any that fail to clock in.

Temperatures are extreme, sizzling above 40 °C in summer while winter nights frequently plummet below zero. January to April are the rainy months, averaging 200 mm per annum — although in some years the rains don't put in an appearance at all.

As I've discovered over the years, the Kalahari has many faces. On one occasion I arrived just after heavy rain had fallen and the place looked like Namaqualand, with flowers everywhere. The next time round, there had been no rain at all. Herds of desperate wildebeest came from Botswana in a hopeless quest for food and water. The winds had dropped, the windmills stood idle, and the waterholes dried up. The wildebeest never stood a chance. To their credit, the rangers left the carcasses where they had fallen — and a new miniature ecosystem developed around each one … with ants, scorpions and other insects living off the remains of each animal, and in turn feeding smaller creatures.

On another visit, I arrived to find that part of the road along the Nossob riverbed had turned into a quagmire as the result of heavy downpours. It took us a whole day to drive our 4-wheel drive vehicle from Twee Rivieren to Nossob, with frequent stops to help the hapless drivers of other vehicles which were stuck in the mud — as well as a great deal of reconnoitring to find the best way northwards.

The dominant features of this Kalahari landscape are the grass-covered orange dunes — the more rain, the more grass — and the usually dry river beds. Probably the two most common trees in the Kalahari are the shepherd's tree, found mainly in the dunes, and the camelthorn tree which is prevalent in the dry river beds.

The tsamma melon is a very important source of both water and food. The plant is a creeper, which grows along the dunes, and bears a large round fruit.

Considering that the region is semi-desert, an amazing variety of animals live here, including carnivores such as lion, cheetah, leopard, spotted and brown hyena and black-backed jackal. You'll also be able to see blue wildebeest, gemsbok (oryx), springbok (in profusion), red hartebeest, African wild cat, caracal, suricate, yellow mongoose, ground squirrel, Cape fox, bat-eared fox, honey badger, porcupine, steenbok and eland. The numbers of wildebeest, hartebeest and eland, fluctuate greatly.

Bird life is prolific, too, with a large variety of raptors including vultures, eagles, hawks, falcons, kestrels, owls, harriers, buzzards and kites. The large, distinctive nests of the sociable

weavers dot the landscape of this area, looking very much like the roofs of badly made thatched cottages.

You'll also come across Namaqua and Burchell's sandgrouse. These enterprising and industrious birds carry water in their breast feathers, for thirsty chicks back in the nest — which can be as much as 50 km from the nearest waterhole. I have often seen these sandgrouses (sandgrice?) at Cubitje Quap (just north of Nossob) and Rooiputs (north of Twee Rivieren).

Please remember that the Kalahari is a malaria area, and it is essential to take the necessary precautions, particularly in summer. Use an insect repellent and talk to your pharmacist about which tablets are the most suitable

(and make a point of taking them as prescribed).

This region has been described in great depth by other writers, and specialist information is readily available for those of you who want it. For non-specialists who are nevertheless ardent nature lovers, I'd like to try and give an impression of what goes through my mind whenever I visit the Kalahari.

Travelling from Johannesburg, via Vryburg, Kuruman, Hotazel and Vanzylsrus, the feeling of anticipation and excitement grows as I get closer — particularly when I leave the tarred road at Hotazel (an aptly named place if there ever was) and head for Twee Rivieren along 330 kilometres of dirt road. (If all that gravel is unappealing, there is an alternative route via Upington; it's about 100 km longer but involves a lot less dust).

After the Molopo Hotel turn-off, the orange dunes start to become more noticeable, especially on the left side of the road, with the houses of the local people on and around the dunes.

In the Kalahari Gemsbok Park, time takes a holiday … no TV, no radio, no newspapers … just the sheer pleasure of being there. I become deeply aware of the complex relationship between the various species of birds and animals, as well as between members of the same species. As sunset approaches, the tik-tik-tik of barking geckos (lizards) punctuates the still evening air — one of the evocative sounds of Africa, epitomising the Kalahari and the Namib. Stress and tension melt away like the morning dew and I feel that my Q.O.L. (quality of life) is significantly enhanced by just being in this magical place.

On a moonless night, in the pollution-free atmosphere, I can think of nothing more vivid or memorable than the overhead canopy of stars. Seen through a good pair of binoculars, they seem startlingly bright and it is all too easy to fall into a reverie, enthralled by the timelessness of the universe.

But instead of relying on my passionate prose, the best bet is to go there yourself, and personally experience the excitement and tranquillity of the Kalahari.

Bookings can be made through the Central Reservations Offices of the South African National Parks Board, at tel. (012) 343-1991 (Pretoria), or (021) 22-2810 (Cape Town).

NAMAQUALAND

Namaqualand — "The Greatest Flower Show on Earth" – straddles the main road between Cape Town and Windhoek, in the north-west Cape between Steinkopf (near Springbok), in the north, and Vanrhynsdorp in the south. August and September are usually the peak months for floral activity, although in some years the flowers have been known to take centre stage as early as the end of July or as late as October. The precise timing depends on when and where the winter rain falls — which makes things awkward for tourists on a schedule, but you just have to take your chances and hope to strike it lucky (few things are more infuriating than the words, "the flowers were wonderful two weeks ago; you should have been here then").

How can I describe the fiesta of colour that is Namaqualand in the spring? The fields spread out like immense and unending tapestries, embroidered with every shade of gold, pink, yellow, blue, purple … tinges of pastels here, splashes of bold colour there, while a variety of muted greens set off the rich tones of the pre-cambrian rock formations in the granite koppies (hills).

The profusion of flowers is amazing. On one occasion I counted sixteen different species in an area of just one square metre! While some flowers, particularly annuals, only open mid-morning and close mid-afternoon, many are open for a longer period in the day.

For me as a photographer, there is as much visual excitement in a single bloom growing bravely out of a rocky crevice as there is in the spectacle of horizon-to-horizon flowers. The permanence and solidity of the koppies and rocks provides a striking counterpoint to the delicacy and fragility of the flowers.

Treat the Namaqualand wild flowers with the same respect that you would give your flower-beds at home, and make an effort not to trample any plants. Exercise your eco-responsibility and remember that other people will want to enjoy and photograph this natural wonderland.

A couple of years ago, the S.A. Nature Foundation bought a farm near the lovely little town of Kamieskroon. Skilpad Nature Reserve, as it is known, has become quite popular, and is gaining a fine reputation for preserving the unique natural heritage of this area.

Photographing among the huge boulders near Steinkopf, or on the Atlantic coast at Hondeklip Bay … or at unspoilt Kamieskroon, with its hospitable little hotel and friendly, informative owners .... or driving over the winding Kamiesberg Pass above Kamieskroon … or standing knee-deep in a carpet of flowers near Nieuwoudtville and Vanrhynsdorp .... wherever I am in Namaqualand in the spring,

I am continually entranced by the indescribable beauty of this magical kingdom — which has been aptly described as "the garden of the gods".

RICHTERSVELD NATIONAL PARK

Proclaimed in 1991, the Richtersveld National Park is unique in that its management is shared by the National Parks Board and the local inhabitants, who continue to live within the borders of the park. This is a mountain desert region south of the Orange River (which forms the border between South Africa and Namibia), and north of Namaqualand, in the north-western Cape.

The Richtersveld is a botanist's paradise, with a large number of plants which are unique to the region. It is also a geologist's idea of heaven, with terrestrial features spanning nearly the whole of the Earth's history.

At the time of writing there is no accommodation in the Richtersveld, although there are several designated camp sites, which boast very little in the way of facilities. A 4-wheel drive vehicle is a necessity, and you are not allowed to leave the roads.

Permits for travelling into the park can be obtained at Sendelingsdrift from the curator. You have to show your permit at the entrance to the Richtersveld National Park, at the Helskloof Gate.

You can approach the Richtersveld, as I did, from the south. Starting at Springbok (on the main road between Cape Town and Windhoek), head north as far as Steinkopf, then westwards on the Port Nolloth road. Keep an eye out for a signboard directing you to turn right onto the dirt road leading to "Eksteenfontein". As you head north, you start to become aware that this is one of the remotest parts of the country.

If you are pressed for time and fancy a route that is definitely faster and easier (but less interesting) you could drive west from Steinkopf as far as Port Nolloth, then head north to Alexander Bay and eastwards to Khubus.

It is imperative to carry an extra spare tyre (by which I mean a spare tyre as well as a spare spare tyre, if you get my drift) and sufficient petrol, water and food for your stay in the Richtersveld. It is also not a bad idea to travel with at least one other vehicle in case of emergencies (and it does no harm if one of your companions happens to be a medical doctor, because there are positively no civilised amenities to be found — which is precisely why the Richtersveld appeals to me in the first place!). There are precious few signposts here,

so you'll need a good map, as well as the ability to read the thing properly. Please take plastic rubbish bags with you, and bring all your garbage out with you again. Ensure that you have a good supply of gas bottles for cooking — you will not be permitted to gather firewood in the park.

Make no mistake about it, this is a harsh and untamed region, but hauntingly beautiful for just that reason. With its huge mountains and deep valleys, the Richtersveld looks like the back of the moon and is one of the most desolate places I have ever been to. The annual rainfall varies between 20 mm and 130 mm — although in some years no rain falls at all. Temperatures are extreme, sometimes rising to 50 °C in summer, while dropping below freezing in the course of a winter night. There is some wildlife in the area, with occasional sightings of steenbok, klipspringer, leopard, jackal, aardwolf, Hartmann's zebra, grey rhebuck, bat-eared fox, caracal, baboon and vervet monkey.

Arguably the Richtersveld is as much part of the Namib Desert as it is part of Namaqualand, and is particularly well known for its large variety of succulents. The most prominent of these is the Halfmens (half-human) — so-called because, with their straight trunks and leafy heads, they sometimes resemble a group of people standing on the crest of a hill. The species is endangered and the Richtersveld is one of the few places where

it occurs. It is also a very slow grower, because of the sparse rainfall. The specimens I saw were more than 2 metres high, so they must have been very old indeed.

Nama herdsmen settled here many years ago, and you'll be able to see their descendants tending their goats in the area.

Campsite bookings for the Richtersveld National Park can be made by dialling (0256) 831-1506 from within South Africa.

KRUGER NATIONAL PARK

Before the turn of the century, the forerunner of what is today world-famous as the Kruger Park was proclaimed, with President Paul Kruger as its main protagonist, despite much opposition at the time. Fortunately for us, his views prevailed, as did his incredible foresight and within thirty years the Park was named after him.

Visitors from the UK might be surprised to discover that the park covers an area the size of Wales (some 2 million hectares), with a length of 350 km and a width that ranges from 50 to 100 km. As you might expect, the variety of scenery and game in various areas of the park is staggering. The accommodation facilities are also excellent.

Recently the fences separating the park from the private game reserves on the western side have come down, providing an even larger area for animals to roam and resume their migratory routes. These private game lodges offer superb facilities — if you can afford them. There is also a possibility that the fences to the north and east (bordering Zimbabwe and Mozambique) might be pulled down at some time in the future.

If you can spare the time, you'll have no difficulty in occupying yourself happily for several weeks in this park, in the Lowveld of the Eastern Transvaal. It is a wildlife paradise, situated conveniently close to the heavily populated region of Gauteng and requires only 4 or 5 hours travelling, on excellent roads.

I prefer to visit the Kruger National Park (or "Kruger" as the locals call it) in winter because the climate at that time is a lot cooler and more comfortable than the searing heat of summer. Also, because most of the rain falls in summer, the winter vegetation is less lush and the animals are consequently easier to spot. However, even if you don't have a choice

as to when you visit the park, go there anyway —game and bird viewing prospects are great at any time of the year.

Don't limit yourself to looking for "the Big Five" (lion, elephant, buffalo, rhino, leopard). There are some 20 species of antelope and about 140 varieties of mammals, and when it comes to bird life, there are literally hundreds of species to look out for.

Before you head for Kruger, arm yourself with a reputable animal field guide and bird book (plus a pair of binoculars, and a camera or video camera) so that you'll know what you're looking at. If you want to follow the animals' spoor on foot and feel a sense of being really close to them, the Kruger National Park offers walking trails from some camps, led by experienced game rangers; at some camps, night drives in open game-viewing vehicles are available. Early booking is advisable for both.

Dawn and dusk are the best viewing times, not only because they provide the best light, but because these are the times when the animals are at their most active and most likely to be seen.

Whenever I spot a bird or animal that I want to photograph, I try and move into the correct photographic position first time. What is the 'correct' position? In general, try to shoot with the sun behind you if possible. Of course, there are other options, like backlighting (for silhouettes) and side-light-

ing, but the important thing is that you should always be aware of the position of the sun as you approach the subject.

Another question that aspirant wildlife photographers often ask is "How close should I get?" Bearing in mind the need to be an observer rather than a participant, the answer is that you should move as close as you can without making the animal or bird uncomfortable about your presence. Never impinge on its "space", stay in your car, and stay on the road. (Remember that these animals are wild and some of them are perfectly capable of having you for dinner if you get too near). The actual distance varies from species to species and what they are doing at the time. Be aware of the animal's reactions to you, which should be minimal.

Whether you travel in the Punda Maria and Shingwedzi region in the north, Letaba, Olifants or Satara in the centre of the park, or Skukuza, Pretoriuskop or Malelane in the south, you are assured of seeing most of what is best in African wildlife. A good detailed map of the Kruger Park is obtainable from each of the shops in the camps.

Four wheel drive vehicles are not necessary, but malaria tablets are.

ADDO ELEPHANT PARK

About 12000 ha in size, this park is situated 70 km from Port Elizabeth in the Eastern Cape. It was proclaimed in 1931, with the objective of preserving both the vegetation and the wildlife, particularly elephant.

There are currently more than 200 elephants in the park, but they're not easy to see because of the dense bush. However, if you're keen eyed and lucky you should be able to find them. You might also see black rhino, buffalo, kudu, grey duiker, Cape grysbok, caracal, suricate and black-backed jackal. Birdlife is plentiful.

While you are there, look out for the flightless dung beetles, which thrive in the park (in fact, there are signboards proclaiming that dung beetles have right of way). These fascinating insects can frequently be seen, using their rear legs to roll a ball of dung many times their size across the road.

Accommodation facilities and roads are excellent. On the restaurant wall you will see the huge mounted head of Hapoor (meaning "bitten ear"), the legendary leader of the Addo elephants for 24 years, until his death in 1968.

MOUNTAIN ZEBRA NATIONAL PARK

This Park, near Cradock, has a real ecological success story to tell. The Mountain Zebra have been brought back from the brink of extinction, to the extent that they now number more than 200, and each year some are transferred to other areas, such as the Karoo National Park. The Mountain Zebra is slightly smaller than the more commonly seen Burchell's Zebra and has a brownish-orange muzzle. There are no

intermediate stripes between the dominant black ones, its dewlap is very noticeable, and the stripes go all the way down the legs.

Other animals which I have seen in this park are red hartebeest, black wildebeest, springbok and blesbok.

If, like me, you enjoy landscapes that seem to go on forever, the views over the Karoo are particularly impressive from the high plateau known as Rooiplaat. This is the area in which the majority of the animals are found. There are also a number of hiking trails of varying lengths for energetic visitors.

On one occasion, while standing in a slight drizzle, I had the fascinating experience of seeing a moonlight rainbow in this park. The colours were not quite as vivid as those of its daytime counterpart, but definitely distinguishable. I can remember seeing the same phenomenon at the Victoria Falls.

The accommodation in the park is good and so are the roads, some of which have been tarred. There is also a restaurant and a swimming pool.

In addition to those which I have described in some detail, there are several other National Parks around the country, each with its own characteristics and charm, and well worth a visit.

They are:-

Tsitsikamma National Park
Bontebok National Park
Karoo National Park
Augrabies Falls National Park
Golden Gate Highland National Park
Langebaan National Park
Tankwa National Park
Marekele National Park
Hei-Gariep National Park

At the confluence of the Auob and Nossob Rivers, just a few kilometres north of Twee Rivieren, this herd of Blue Wildebeest were kicking up a storm of dust, which glowed like a fire in the rising sun. Although wildebeest calves can stand up and run minutes after birth, they suffer a heavy mortality rate at the mercy of numerous carnivores.

I saw this Bateleur Eagle at the delightfully-named waterhole called Cubitje Quap, just north of the Nossob Camp. I'm no linguist, but I believe that *bateleur* is the French word for an acrobat, which is not much help in explaining the origin of the name. It may have something to do with the bird's flight pattern, which is rather like a cross between a tightrope walker and a stealth bomber (all wing and very little tail).

The big and the small. The Martial Eagle *(left)* is one of Southern Africa's largest raptors, here seen sitting atop a huge Sociable Weaver's nest. The smallest raptor, a Pygmy Falcon *(above)*, brings home a tasty lizard for its chicks, which are safely housed in the same nest. Pygmy Falcons often take over part of a Sociable Weaver's nest, which in itself can house up to 300 of these small birds.

Despite its ability to achieve a top speed of more than 100 k.p.h., the Cheetah is far from being an efficient hunter — with a success rate of only 20%. This specimen was photographed in full flight, while a herd of Springbok *(right)* grazed nearby in blissful ignorance.

A successful Cheetah "kill"
(this page and opposite).

A Springbok *(right)* "pronks" in its efforts to evade the hunter. The characteristic stiff-legged leap derives its name from an Afrikaans word meaning "to show off or strut as if on parade".

With military precision, the hunters carry out an elaborate pincer movement, culminating in the capture of their prey *(left and below)*.

A pair of Jackals, who don't exactly see eye to eye on the matter, squabble over scraps left by the Cheetah *(below)*.

The mother Cheetah shares the trophy with her cubs *(above)*.

The Secretary Bird builds its nest on the top of a tree, in this case the camelthorn tree. While they roost at night, most of the day is spent stalking through the veld. They are adept at catching snakes, which are no match for their razor-sharp talons.

I have spent many happy hours watching and photographing the Suricate (Meerkat).

The sentry on the right keeps a wary eye open for Jackals and other predators, while the rest of the family forages for food or basks in the sunlight. The Suricate on the left, at the mouth of its hole in the ground, keeps a watchful eye on the sky — raptors regard this creature as a tasty meal. On the ground, however, scorpions and snakes are no match for these agile little animals.

The Cape Fox is the only true fox in Southern Africa. I saw this fellow early one morning, close to his den in the ground. The long bushy tail and distinctive foxy features make it easy to distinguish this species from the black-backed jackal — even at a distance.

Like the Suricates, these Ground Squirrels live underground, and the entrance holes of these two species look very similar. A distinctive feature of this little Kalahari creature is the bushy tail, which it uses as a parasol to protect it from the sun on hot days.

The Black-backed Jackal is the arch opportunist of the Kalahari. I have seen them harry young Springbok, snatch birds out of the air, steal part of a Lion's kill and follow Cheetah at a discreet distance. Jackals are omnivores, and will eat a large variety of foods — although meat is still their first choice.

The two most common species of antelope in the Kalahari are the Gemsbok (Oryx) and the Springbok. They are found on the dunes and in the dry river bed. On one occasion I observed a herd of over 2 000 Springbok trekking along the Auob River. Both these antelope are browsers and grazers, and both can survive on surprisingly little water.

A pair of Secretary Birds go through their mating ritual.

Most people have a soft spot for cute and cuddly young animals. In the real world, a Lion cub in the Kalahari faces an uncertain future, and only one in every five are likely to reach adulthood.

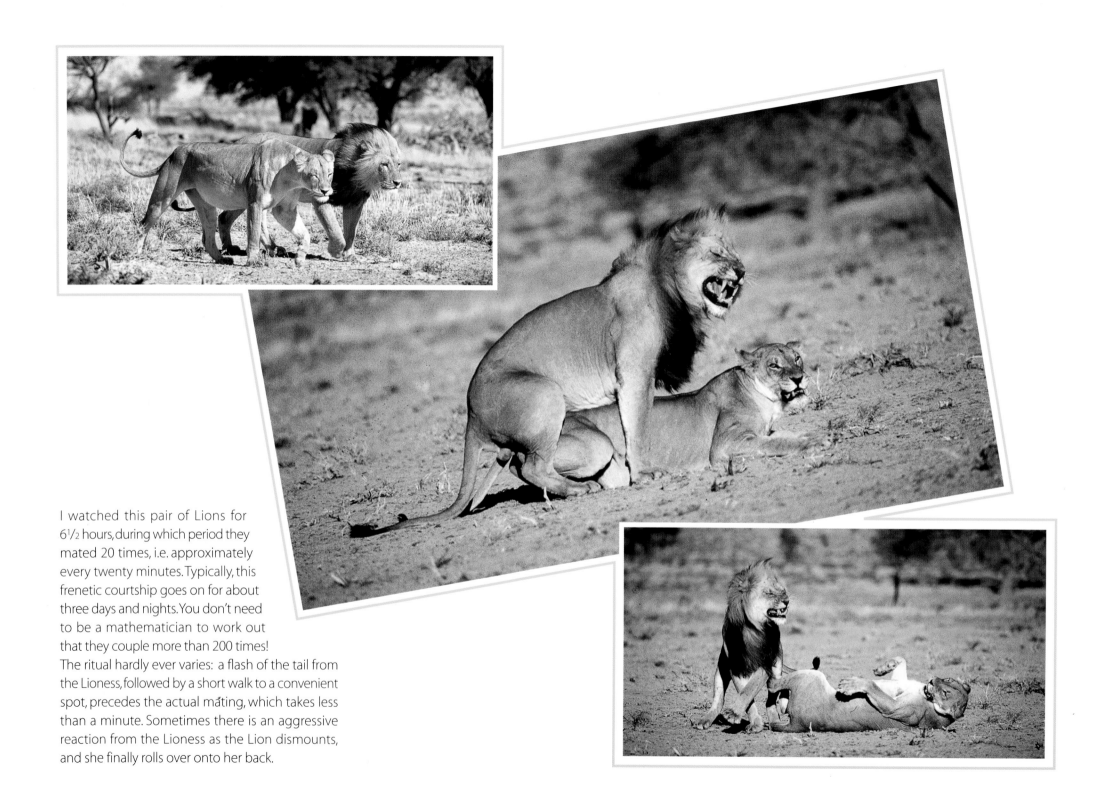

I watched this pair of Lions for 6½ hours, during which period they mated 20 times, i.e. approximately every twenty minutes. Typically, this frenetic courtship goes on for about three days and nights. You don't need to be a mathematician to work out that they couple more than 200 times! The ritual hardly ever varies: a flash of the tail from the Lioness, followed by a short walk to a convenient spot, precedes the actual mating, which takes less than a minute. Sometimes there is an aggressive reaction from the Lioness as the Lion dismounts, and she finally rolls over onto her back.

Lion cubs often fall prey to Hyena while their parents are out hunting. Many of them also starve, especially during droughts when food sources are scarce. Incredibly, the Porcupine — despite its dangerous quills — is highly regarded as a delicacy by the Kalahari Lion.

The sunset silhouette *(main picture)* was taken near Nossob, when one Lioness in a group of seven deigned to raise her head for the photographer.

A magnificent flower carpet of Namaqualand daisies intermingled with many other species, provides a beautiful natural garden for this old farmhouse.

The Kalkoentjiebos *(left)* is sometimes used for medicinal purposes, and is reputedly a remedy for influenza and stomach ailments. Some people believe that it can cure cancer. On the opposite page *(main picture)* a kokerboom (quiver tree) grows amongst the flowers on a rocky slope.

(Left) A crevice in the Pre-Cambrian rock provides a home for Namaqualand daisies, while *(right)* a rocky outcrop towers over contrasting mauve and yellow flowers. *(Main picture)* A vivid splash of colour on a farm near Nieuwoudtville, in the South of Namaqualand.

A small house *(left)* nestles among Namaqualand daisies. *(Above)* Two local ladies in characteristic dress pass the time of day on the front steps of their house, which has been painted in colours inspired by the landscape.

The Orange River marks the border between Namibia and South Africa. This is the De Hoop campsite, in the Richtersveld. Other campsites in the area are Pooitjespram, Richtersberg, Kokerboomkloof and De Koei.

(This page) Three contrasting Half-mens plants *(Pachypodium Namaquanum)* eke out an existence on a mountain in the Richtersveld. This plant is an endangered species and should never be removed. *(Main picture, right)* The struggle for survival is epitomised by this hardy tree scrabbling for a toe-hold at the very top of a mountain.

(Left) The relatively scarce Baster Kokerboom (Aloe Pilansii) is much taller (up to 9 metres) than the more common Kokerboom, but generally with fewer branches and leaves.

The star trails (top) are the result of a 5-hour time exposure of the night sky, with the camera mounted on a tripod. The four bright streaks on the right are the Southern Cross, while the centre of the circle represents due south. The mountains of the Richtersveld provide the silhouetted foreground. I understand that the various colours of the stars are an indication of their ages.

Arguably one of the most colourful and beautiful birds in Southern Africa, this Lilac-Breasted Roller was photographed in cold weather — hence its fluffed-up feathers. Possibly because it was freezing cold, this bird was most accommodating and even turned round to enable me to photograph its other side.

This White Rhino (Square-lipped Rhinoceros) was one of a group of seven photographed in thick bush. It differs from the Black Rhino in several ways. The White Rhino is bigger and has a square-shaped lip, with a pronounced hump on the back of its neck. It is also a grazer, as opposed to the Black Rhino which is more of a browser. I hope you'll agree that his horn looks better on him, rather than being put to questionable use elsewhere!

Definitely my favourite animals! These two young Cheetah were waiting obediently on an anthill near Dulini, as instructed by their mother. Soon after this shot was taken they moved off on a signal from their mother, who had just killed an Impala.

These Buffalo had been seriously harried by a large pride of Lion in the area, causing them to spend the night in a circular "laager" formation, all facing outwards. Notice the Red-Billed Oxpeckers stealing a ride — and a meal — on their hosts.

This Lion caused great consternation among a large herd of Buffalo late one afternoon, near Shingwedzi. He was deliberately provocative, lying in the middle of the road in clear view of the herd. I can't be sure that a kill was achieved during the night, but it seems highly likely.

This Saddle-billed Stork *(above)* was one of several that I saw wading around in a small pool near Nwanetsi. They caught several frogs, but also lost most of them as a result of squabbling over the catch.

While crossing the Letaba River bridge I chanced to look down and saw this Great White Egret *(left)* on the river bank. This is one of my favourite photographs … it relates the bird to its environment and, on a visual level, displays an interesting tension between the off-centre subject and the curve of the river bank.

The Yellow-billed Hornbill *(opposite)* has — rather self-evidently — a prominent yellow bill, which distinguishes it from other Hornbills. They are a common sight in the Kruger National Park, where they can often be seen gliding from one tree to the next.

This Red-billed Oxpecker *(left)* here seen clinging to the flank of a Giraffe, can also often be seen on Buffalo and various species of Antelope.

(Top) Three small Tree Squirrels sunning themselves in the early morning, near Shingwedzi. They are strictly diurnal, and have their nests in trees, although they spend considerable time foraging on the ground.

Shortly before sunset, I turned a corner in the Addo Elephant Park and came across this elephant mother and her calf, right next to the road.
Most of the time the mother positioned herself between me and her baby; it is this kind of caring behaviour which endears us to this species.

(Top left) The thickness of the bush in the Addo Elephant Park is well illustrated here, as the baby strides out ahead of its mother who has stopped to browse.

(Bottom left) An Elephant family enjoys a mud bath and a mid-morning drink.

(Opposite) The brown muzzle and the lack of intermediate stripes on this Mountain Zebra are shown clearly in this photograph.

(Technical note: The camera's built-in meter would tend to overexpose a scene like this, because of the dark background. The remedy is to close down by $\frac{1}{2}$ to 1 stop).

On the high plateau of Rooiplaat, a Mountain Zebra stands out majestically against the dark mountain backdrop.

The Red Hartebeest in shadow makes a striking silhouette in this Karoo landscape. These fleet-footed animals rarely have to drink water, and obtain moisture from the food they eat.

A photographer's paradise … the pastel lilacs and deep indigo tones of the Karoo at sunset.

There's a rule in photography which is "Use ƒ8 — and be there!" The best photographs can often be made at a time when other people are asleep in bed. In this dawn shot, the first rays of sunlight catch the early morning mist rising from the valley below.

BOTSWANA

CHOBE
NATIONAL
PARK

OKAVANGO
DELTA

MOREMI

NXAI PAN

MAUN

MAKGADIGADI PANS

FRANCISTOWN

BOTSWANA

GABORONE

BOTSWANA
BOTSWANA
BOTSWANA
BOTSWANA
BOTSWANA
BOTSWANA
BOTSWANA
BOTSWANA
SWANA

MAKGADIGADI PANS

Just south of the tarred road between Nata and Maun lies the Makgadigadi Pans National Park. If you enjoy living under canvas … that's good, because there are campsites but no other accommodation. This National Park forms a very small part of the Makgadigadi Salt Pans in the Central District of Botswana (comprising the Ntwetwe Pan in the west and the Sowa Pans in the east).

This vast area, with its featureless horizons and dazzlingly bright cracked mud pans, is a dry thirst-land for most of the time … although I visited the Makgadigadi a few years ago after a heavy rainfall and it had turned into a vast lake, just a few centimetres deep, packed with flamingoes and pelicans.

Another way of viewing these endless horizons is to visit the Nata Sanctuary, roughly 10 km south of the village of Nata. Here you can drive right up to the edge of the pan in a conventional 2-wheel drive vehicle. For the more adventurous, there are a couple of tracks in the pan itself, but a 4-wheel drive would be a good idea. Don't try driving off the tracks, though, because the pan itself can be soft underneath the crusty surface.

You'll be able to find comfortable accommodation at Nata Lodge, just a few kilometres away on the main road. It is quite often heavily booked, so prior reservation is recommended. Just north of the Nata–Maun road lies the Nxai Pan. This pan is most famous for its Baines' Baobabs (enormous indigenous trees made famous by the artist Thomas Baines, who depicted them more than 130 years ago). I believe that visitors are no longer permitted to stay overnight at the campsite nearby.

OKAVANGO DELTA

Most visitors to the Okavango first see the Delta from the air. From a small plane, here's what will strike you:

1. The flatness of the landscape.
2. The interesting mixture of land and water.
3. The extent of wildlife, all easily visible from the air … herds of elephant, wildebeest, impala or lechwe, as well as buffalo and giraffe.
4. Channels in the water, caused by mekoro (dugout canoes), as they make their way slowly through the reeds and waterlilies.
5. Whether or not you share my apprehension about flying in small aeroplanes, you'll certainly be impressed by the obvious competence, friendliness and helpfulness of the pilots.
6. The runways look so small and uneven from the air, yet they are really quite adequate when you get closer.
7. You really feel part of nature up there — especially if you're fortunate enough to see a vulture float past.
8. A sense of eager anticipation at what you can expect when you arrive … game viewing, camps with an indefinable feel of the "real" Africa, the hospitality, and of course the getting-away-from-it-all feeling that comes from being in a wildlife paradise.

The Okavango River starts in the highlands of Angola, flows south-east into Botswana (where it spreads out to form the delta) — and then dries up in the sands of the Kalahari, without ever reaching the sea. It takes a good five months for the water to flow from the Angolan border to the town of Maun, in Botswana.

The Okavango Delta is one of the few areas in Southern African where you really do need good guides to assist in finding your way about, and to provide the necessary transportation, whether on land or on water. In Maun you will find many fine safari companies who are geared up to fly you into the delta region by light aircraft, which is probably the best way to go there. After that you can explore the Delta from mekoro (those dugout canoes I was referring to earlier), from houseboats (in some areas), or safari vehicles. I've had personal

experience using Wilderness Safaris, whom I can recommend.

Because of the abundance of water in the delta, insects are an ever-present hazard. It is essential to take anti-malaria tablets (starting before you enter the area). Consult a pharmacist about the correct type and any possible side-effects. Think about other anti-mosquito measures, too, such as repellents, mosquito netting and mosquito coils. You'll also need to take precautions against the tsetse fly, which can inflict a painful and itchy bite even through jeans, thick jerseys and several layers of clothing. (According to experienced travellers in the area, you should wear light-coloured clothes; apparently tsetse flies prefer dark colours — especially blue).

The delta is a wonderful combination of big and small islands dotted around reed-filled water, which drifts languorously to the south.

The islands — just a metre or two above the water level — are mostly covered in lush vegetation, such as fan palms.

One of the first things you'll notice about the delta is the crystal clarity of the water, with no sediment whatsoever. There is nothing quite as relaxing as being poled through them in absolute silence, watching the fish eagles perched on the surrounding trees, and the red lechwe running through the water. You'll also be able to see birds like the African jacana, pygmy goose, reed warblers, bee-eaters, egrets, herons, and

cormorants. There is also a wide variety of frogs and spiders. If you are very lucky you might see an elusive sitatunga buck.

I recall two very memorable experiences in the delta — neither of which I was able to photograph, although my wife video-taped the first of these. We were out on a game drive one night. As the spotlight circled over the river all we could see were dozens of eyes staring at us from the water. It soon became obvious that the area was teeming with crocodiles. A little further up the channel we came across a great churning in the water, as countless crocodiles — including the biggest I have ever seen — devoured a zebra carcass in the water.

The other never-to-be-forgotten experience occurred one evening at the Mombo Camp (run by Wilderness Safaris), when we were within earshot of a battle between several spotted hyena. These animals make a greater variety of sounds than almost any other species, and for virtually the whole night we were "privileged" to hear the hyenas' full repertoire of whoops, cackles, and screams from very close quarters. As you might guess, nobody slept much that night. Next morning we found a dead hyena no more than 50 metres from our tent.

MOREMI GAME RESERVE

Before you head north from Maun in the direction of Moremi and Chobe — do your homework! Make sure that you have enough petrol, water and food, because there is nothing available until you reach Kasane, on the Chobe River. Here, as in the Kaokoveld and the

Certainly the biggest Baobab I've ever seen. This giant specimen, in the Okavango, dwarfs the group of birdwatchers walking under its massive branches.

Richtersveld, I start with 300 litres of petrol, 100 litres of water, and enough food for a month. Incidentally, I make a practice of taking water from home, simply because I know that my stomach (and palate) can handle it! Local water is an unknown factor in Botswana, and there is nothing worse than picking up a tummy bug when you're a long way from home. As I said, do your preparation thoroughly and save yourself embarrassment — or disaster — later.

While you can certainly travel from Maun to Savuti in a day, I really urge you to spare the time to visit Moremi. You'll find this wonderful reserve a little to the west of the "main road", and it would be a crying shame to bypass it.

The Moremi Game Reserve comprises part of the eastern section of the Okavango Delta. The best way to get there, if you have your own transportation, is by 4-wheel drive vehicle from Maun. I have encountered quite thick sand on the roads in places, which in the rainy season (summer) can become almost impassable. Some 70 km north of Maun you'll find a "Moremi" sign marking a turnoff to the left. The southern entrance into the Game Reserve is via the Maqwee Gate, also known as South Gate, 100 km north of Maun.

Moremi stretches across dry and wet areas in a rich tapestry of mopane woodland, islands, flood plains, rivers and lagoons. Many of the islands are small, but Chief's Island, in

the west of the reserve, is massive and magnificent. Here you'll be able to view everything that is best in African wild life, including the endangered African wild dog. I have walked and ridden around parts of this island, and I found it to be an experience I will never forget.

An astonishing variety and volume of wildlife awaits you in the Moremi Game Reserve. We saw huge herds of elephant and buffalo, large numbers of beautiful sable antelope, hippo, lion, wildebeest, zebra, kudu, giraffe, red lechwe and impala, and an amazing variety of bird life.

We pitched our tents at the Xakanaxa camping site, right on the water's edge, where we received frequent nocturnal visits from elephant, buffalo and hippo. There are no fences around the campsites, so it is worth remembering that this is an animal kingdom, and that we are the intruders. Take care, especially at night.

Moremi is shaped like a triangle, with Maqwee campsite in the south. Third Bridge campsite is in the west, with the Khwai Camping site near the North Gate in the east, and Xakanaxa between them. The facilities are fairly basic, and the sites can sometimes be a little overcrowded, especially during school holidays.

You'll also be able to stay at a number of excellent private game lodges in Moremi. For more information, talk to your travel agent.

Here are some useful suggestions when you visit the Moremi Game Reserve:-

1. The speed limit is a fairly laid-back 40 kph — with good reason. Speeding is dangerous to animals, other visitors and yourselves. Dust inhibits the growth of roadside vegetation. So relax, and enjoy better game-viewing at slower speeds. Another good reason for travelling slowly is that very often sticks and small logs of wood are left in the road by motorists who used them to extricate themselves from the mud or sand. You can well imagine the kind of tyre damage that this debris could cause.

2. Keep to the roads. Flood plain vegetation is extremely susceptible to damage by trampling. Driving off the road could also result in your being stranded without help.

3. Night driving is strictly prohibited.

4. Camp only at designated sites.

5. Extinguish camp fires — and do not litter.

6. Do not remove any living or other objects. However, you are allowed to gather firewood for use in the reserve.

7. Although you might be tempted, do not feed the animals. They lose their fear of humans, thus becoming a nuisance and dangerous, and many have had to be destroyed in the past. Oranges in particular should not even be brought into the reserve, as the elephants react strongly to the smell.

8. Do not harass or attempt to "play" with the animals. They can be very dangerous, especially when they feel threatened.

9. Swimming is dangerous. It is allowed at Third Bridge only. If you must swim, keep very close to the bridge and avoid taking your dip at dawn, dusk or at night. In all other areas swimming is prohibited. Remember that hippo, crocodile and bilharzia snails (which can cause a debilitating and life-threatening disease) inhabit these waters.

10. Fish only at designated sites. There are crocodiles and hippo out there — and they can move fast!

11. Sleeping outside is very dangerous, even next to a fire. It is not a reliable deterrent — I once saw a hyena delicately lifting a piece of meat out of the still glowing embers.

12. Never leave the campsite unattended. Nimble-fingered baboons and monkeys can open tents, trunks and fridges. Also bear in mind that hyenas eat anything, especially smelly shoes. I remember a hyena that ran off with a cooler box in its mouth (it was never found).

CHOBE NATIONAL PARK

After leaving Moremi through the North Gate, over a very rickety bridge, head north towards Savuti camp, which lies approximately 100 km north of Moremi and is one of five public campsites in the Chobe National Park.

This is definitely 4x4 territory. The route to Savuti crosses the Magwikwe Sand Ridge, and in the rainy season this road would be totally impassable. In stark contrast to Moremi, the landscape on the route to Savuti is much dryer, with less vegetation, but nevertheless uniquely beautiful.

The five public campsites in Chobe are Savuti, Serondela, Linyanti, Nogatsaa and Tshinga, although I believe Serondela will be closed shortly, and a new campsite to the west, close to the Ihaha Loop, will be opened. I would describe them as "barely adequate" — elephant are rather destructive when it comes to ablution facilities!

In addition to the public campsites, there are a number of private game lodges in the Savuti area, situated on the Savuti Channel (which has not reached the Savuti campsite area for many years).

If you're looking for more comfort than you'll find at Serondela, try the lodges close to the town of Kasane, a few kilometres outside Chobe National Park on the south bank of the Chobe River. Look for Kubu Lodge, Cresta Mowana Safari Lodge, Chobe Chilwero and Chobe Safari Lodge.

I have stayed at the Chobe Safari Lodge and found it very comfortable indeed. There are well-appointed bungalows, a camping and caravan site in the grounds, a swimming pool, dining room, lounge, bar and a double-decker barge to take you up the Chobe River on a sunset cruise.

For a touch of real luxury, you should consider the 5-star Chobe Game Lodge, which is situated inside the Chobe National Park. This moorish-styled lodge (overlooking the Chobe River) has played host to many famous guests, including Richard Burton and Elizabeth Taylor, on their second honeymoon.

In northern Botswana, there is a constant migratory movement of animals. During the dry winter months large herds of elephant and buffalo trek northwards towards the rivers. When the rains come to the Savuti region, there are amazingly large herds of zebra, followed closely by predators, particularly south-bound prides of lion.

Near Serondela, the Chobe River flows like a blue ribbon through the green and brown countryside, positively lush when compared with Savuti. The region teems with animals and birds. The roads are good here, and, as long as you stay close to the Chobe River, a 4x4 vehicle is not necessary. In my experience the Chobe National Park (especially near Serondela) is one of the most beautiful — and certainly one of the most photogenic — game-viewing areas in Southern Africa. It is easily accessible from other areas in Botswana, from South Africa, and from the Victoria Falls region of Zimbabwe, a short distance away, with a tarred road right up to Kasane.

The park fees in Botswana are fairly expensive when compared with those in neighbouring countries, and the facilities are not as good; it is nevertheless a superb region to visit, especially for game viewing and photography. Remember, though, that Chobe is a malaria-endemic area and it is advisable to take all the necessary precautions.

Information on Moremi and Chobe is available from Botswana's Department of Wildlife and National Parks in Gaborone, at telephone (09267) 37-1405

To conclude this section, it might be useful to compare the game-viewing situations in both South Africa and Botswana.

The main similarity between the two countries is that they offer excellent opportunities for viewing game in profusion. The facilities (including accommodation, transportation, game-viewing and service) provided by private game lodges and safari companies in both countries are superb in every way.

However, when it comes to facilities for the general public, the similarity ends. In South Africa — with the exception of the limited facilities of the Richtersveld, the National Parks provide comfortable accommodation at reasonable rates, with good roads (4x4 vehicles are not necessary).

In contrast, Botswana's facilities are much more basic, suited more for the really adventurous. 4x4 vehicles are essential, and you must bring your own camping equipment. Botswana's National Parks are relatively more expensive in terms of what they offer. Nevertheless, visits to Botswana's National Parks are unforgettable, with excellent game viewing opportunities. In the end, I suppose, it is a question of "horses for courses". If you enjoy roughing it, then you'll love the Botswana experience. If you enjoy your creature comforts, either put yourself in the hands of a safari company or stick to the more accessible and comfortable South African wildlife experience.

A watch-tower in the Nata Sanctuary, on the edge of the Pan.

Nature's mosaic! A wide-angle lens on the camera (mounted on a tripod, of course) with an exposure of 1/15 second at f22, provides the necessary depth of field for this photograph in the Makgadigadi Pans near Nata. *(Inset)* The same area, a few years ago, covered ankle-deep in water.

A tranquil scene as the sun goes down over the Okavango Delta.

Africa's most efficient hunter, the African Wild Dog, with a success rate of almost 90%, is also its most endangered predator. Subject to canine diseases and the ravages of man, its numbers have been seriously depleted in recent years.
(Inset) Part of a large pack of 34 Wild Dogs hunting Impala and Red Lechwe in the Delta. They brought down one of each in the assault, and quickly devoured them, before several Hyena arrived on the scene.

A Red Lechwe in top gear tries to avoid the attentions of Wild Dogs *(see left)*. This particular animal was in fact brought down soon after the picture was taken.

If you're in a mokoro (dug-out canoe) the best way to handle a Hippo is … very cautiously indeed! Not for nothing are they known as one of Africa's most dangerous animals. On land, it is not a good idea to be trapped between a Hippo and the water.

(Main picture, right) I preferred not to hang around and see if this was a mock charge or the real thing! One photograph from about 30 metres was all I could manage.

The cry of the Fish Eagle … one of Africa's most evocative sounds. These birds are very common in the Okavango Delta, and the thrill of watching one swoop, catch a fish in its talons and soar into the air again is the most adrenalin-pumping experience in the African wilderness.

The Leguaan (or Nile Monitor) is a 2-metre lizard which — despite its apparent ponderousness — can move with surprising speed both in water and on land. It feeds on the eggs of crocodiles and birds, and dives in the water to catch fish and frogs.

(Above) A Chacma Baboon suns itself amid the autumnal colours in the Moremi Game Reserve.

(Inset) An inquisitive young Chacma Baboon clambers over a rock for a better view of the photographer.

Baboons are very sociable creatures, sometimes living in troops of up to a hundred animals, with a particularly strict hierarchy. Every individual knows its place in the general order of things. Here, a curious baby stares at the camera, while the adults unconcernedly groom each other.

There are several varieties of Bee-Eaters in Northern Botswana. On the left we have a Little Bee-Eater while *(right)* a Carmine Bee-Eater provides a splash of colour against the clear blue African sky.

You know you're having a good day when, in the same picture, you photograph a Fish Eagle *and* a herd of Elephant on the banks of the Chobe River, near the Serondela campsite.

(*Far left*) An alert Impala on the Chobe River .

(*Left*) An Elephant mingles with a herd of Impala.

(*Above*) In a single day, each Elephant can drink as much as 200 litres of water and eat 200 kg of food.

(*Main photo, opposite*) A watchful mother Elephant escorts her babies along the bank of the Chobe River. Baby Elephants weigh approximately 120 kg at birth, which occurs after a gestation period of 22 months. An Elephant lives to about 60 years of age.

The photographs on this double-page spread and the next were taken on the bank of the Chobe River. This is what happened: a pride of more than twenty Lion chased and panicked a herd of thirty Buffalo into the river. The Buffalo all drowned. The Lions then pulled them out of the river and onto the bank. They stored most of them in shady places under the bushes, and alternately ate and guarded their kill. Vultures, Marabou Stork, Jackal and Hyena were in close attendance. One vulture became too cheeky and paid the ultimate price.

Sunsets in Northern Botswana are phenomenal! For a stunning photograph you just need something interesting silhouetted in the foreground, whether it be Marabou Stork in a tree *(above)* or a herd of Giraffe *(right)*.

How have the mighty fallen! At one point I counted fourteen Lion on this Elephant carcass. A little later about twenty Spotted Hyena tried unsuccessfully to drive the Lions away from this gargantuan banquet.

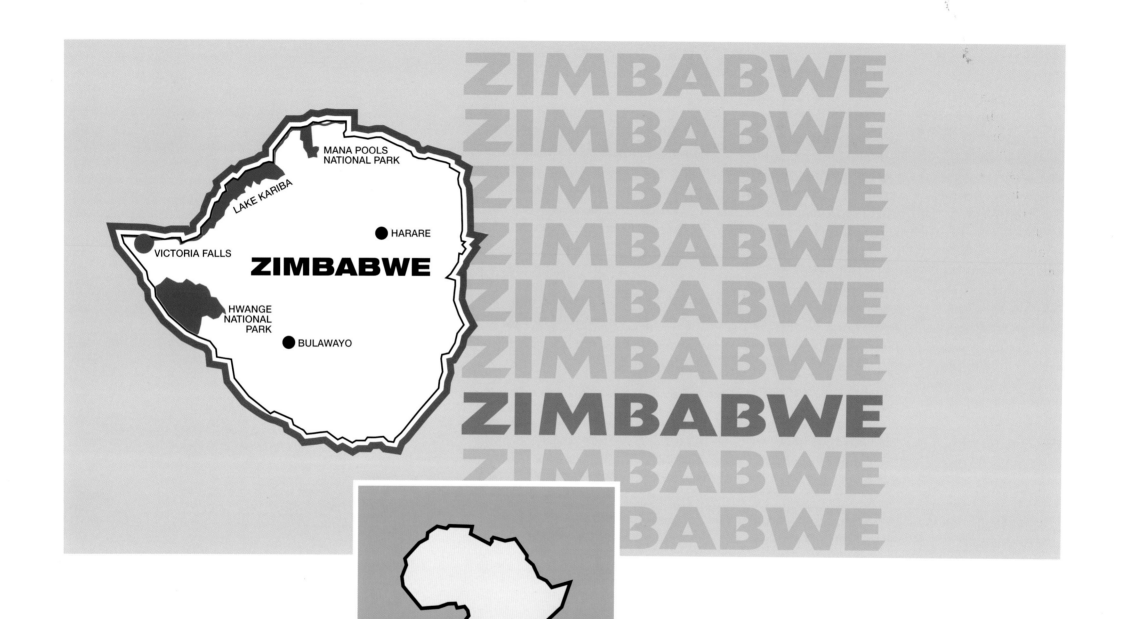

MANA POOLS
NATIONAL PARK

LAKE KARIBA

VICTORIA FALLS

HARARE

ZIMBABWE

HWANGE
NATIONAL
PARK

BULAWAYO

ZIMBABWE
ZIMBABWE
ZIMBABWE
ZIMBABWE
ZIMBABWE
ZIMBABWE
ZIMBABWE
ZIMBABWE
BABWE

VICTORIA FALLS

The Victoria Falls in Western Zimbabwe are an hour's drive from the Botswana border, and rank as one of the Natural Wonders of the World. "The smoke that thunders" is an impressive sight, regardless of the volume of water in the Zambezi River at the time.

Around March and April each year (the end of the rainy season), the river is in full spate. The flow gradually decreases throughout the year until November and December, when the rainy season starts again. While the Victoria Falls is at its most impressive in early April, visibility is at its worst because of the heavy spray (which sometimes soars 300 metres into the air). Obviously the flow varies from year to year, depending on the rains, but I have found that May or June is a good time to visit the falls, when the spray is less dense. The weather is also cooler and less humid than in the summer months. Generally speaking, game viewing is also more comfortable and rewarding.

The falls are almost two kilometres wide and plunge about 100 metres into the gorge below. The river then thunders and lurches through a zig-zag pattern of gorges for a further eight to ten kilometres.

Follow the path from the "Devil's Cataract" through to the bridge between Zimbabwe and Zambia, with all its viewpoints of the falls, and you will experience one of the most scenic walks in the world.

Other activities at the falls, especially for adventurous types, include white water rafting and bungee jumping from the bridge. This is reputed to be one of the longest bungee jumps in the world (although I can't vouch for this fact from personal experience!).

The gorge below the falls provides what is arguably the best one-day white-water rafting adventure in the world. Definitely not for the faint-hearted, with several grade-five rapids to contend with. From the Zimbabwean side of the river, Shearwater is the oldest and best known organisation to offer white-water excursions. Its office is located in the town of Victoria Falls.

If you have the stamina, you could try walking down to the river. Set out from the Victoria Falls Hotel — but remember that you must have a guide. For keen photographers this is about the only way to photograph white-water rafting from dry land, without actually dunking your photographic equipment and putting a severe strain on your insurance policy.

There are also several game reserves in the area, as well as a crocodile ranch, Zambezi River cruises, and a superb golf course (designed by Gary Player) at Elephant Hills Hotel.

I think the ultimate way to view this natural wonder is by flying over the falls. Local operators offer flights in light aircraft, helicopters and micro-lights.

The area boasts a number of very comfortable hotels, ranging from 2-star to 5-star. There is also a large camping/caravan site in the centre of the town, within walking distance of the falls. The Zambezi

National Park just outside the town of Victoria Falls also offers accommodation.

As with many tourist destinations in Southern Africa, the volume of visitors is threatening to harm the pristine beauty of the Victoria Falls and its environment. The need exists for greater control over tour operators and tourist attractions on the river (and other activities near the falls) so as to preserve the natural wonder and beauty of the place for future generations.

HWANGE NATIONAL PARK

The Hwange National Park in western Zimbabwe, covering an area of more than 14 000 square kilometres, has Botswana as its south-western boundary. It is just two hours' drive from the Victoria Falls, and an equal distance from the southern tip of the Kariba Dam. Roads are generally quite good, being either tarred or gravel, and a 4-wheel drive vehicle is not necessary. A network of 500 km of road spreads across the northern section of the park.

There are three large public camps and several smaller ones in the park. Robins Camp

is in the north-west, Sinamatella in the centre, and Main Camp in the north-east, as well as quite a number of excellent private lodges. A vast area in the south of the park, bordering Botswana, has been left virtually untouched by human hands.

Game abounds in huge concentrations, with all the large carnivores, as well as elephant, buffalo, hippo and many species of antelope. More than 400 species of bird life inhabit the region.

In general, I find that the area around Main Camp is best for game viewing and photography, mostly because the vegetation is not as dense as it is in the area around Robin's Camp. Sinamatella is a beautiful camp situated on top of a koppie (hill) with superb views in all directions.

Just outside Robin's Camp are a few cottages, which comprise a camp called

Nantwich. Beautifully situated on top of a hill overlooking two waterholes, it is well worth an overnight stay, if you can get accommodation there.

A waterhole which bears specific mention glories in the name of Nyamandhlovu, close to Main Camp in the east. It boasts a viewing platform from which you will be able to see an incredible variety of game when the animals come down to the waterhole to drink. You can also view game at night, by the eerie glow of a full moon.

Hwange is a malaria area, and I must emphasise once more how important it is for you to take appropriate precautions. Bookings for all Zimbabwe's National Parks can be made through the Zimbabwe National Parks Central Reservations Office in Harare, telephone Harare 726089, or by writing to P.O. Box 8365, Causeway, Harare, Zimbabwe.

LAKE KARIBA

Five hundred kilometres downstream from the Victoria Falls, a gigantic concrete wall blocks the path of the Zambezi River, to form the Kariba Dam — reputedly one of the largest man-made lakes in the world. The dam has drastically altered the ecology of the whole

area since its inauguration in 1960. It created the necessity for "Operation Noah", a huge rescue operation mounted by Rupert Fothergill and his rangers to save thousands of animals which were trapped on small islands by the rising waters (appropriately, the word Kariba means "a trap"). In acknowledgment of this heroic mission, Fothergill Island, a short distance from the town of Kariba, was named after him.

The dam is about 300 km long, with an average width of 30 km. A voyage on the Kariba ferry from Mlibizi to the town of Kariba takes about 22 hours. You could spend a very pleasant evening at the Mlibizi Lodge before boarding the ferry. Then relax and enjoy a comfortable cruise along the length of Lake Kariba. It certainly makes a welcome break from driving, especially if you are blessed with good weather and calm water — as we were. On the ferry, they served a local delicacy which I had not tasted before, something called kapenta. These are small, sardine-like fish, slightly curried, and served with savoury biscuits. Very tasty!

Game viewing in the Kariba area is excellent. There are a couple of National Parks: Chizarira (which is largely underdeveloped) and Matusadona (which has a number of lodges and some campsites). A 4x4 vehicle is recommended. Block bookings only — for the lodges — can be made at the National Park Central Reservations Office in Harare. The luxurious Bumi Hills Lodge, on the western

boundary of the Matusadona National Park, is a superb safari lodge, from which game drives and cruises on the lake are organised. There are also a number of other private safari lodges in the vicinity, and some very fine hotels in the town of Kariba itself.

Then there are the two islands, close to the town of Kariba, Fothergill and Spurwing, both of which boast excellent lodges. The game viewing on these two islands is outstanding.

Or how about game-spotting by houseboat? At the town of Kariba there is a wide choice of these water-craft, from upmarket to … well … adequate. Plan to spend several days on one of these boats, viewing elephant, buffalo, hippo, crocodile, lion (if you're lucky), many species

Right inside the campsite at Mana Pools. Just metres away from my tent, this elephant was plucking leaves from the higher branches of a tree — under the watchful eye of a fellow camper.

of antelope and a wide variety of birds. It's the ultimate wildlife experience. You could also try your hand at a spot of game-fishing; believe me, it is hard to beat the thrill of catching a large tigerfish on Lake Kariba.

If your time or funds are limited, a motorboat day trip to these islands is probably the next best alternative.

MANA POOLS

The Mana Pools National Park in the Zambezi Valley borders on Zambia's Lower Zambezi National Park, and is just a couple of hours north-east of the town of Kariba. The roads are all gravel — but in reasonable condition, except during the rainy season. Four-wheel drive vehicles are not a necessity.

To enter the park, you'll need a permit, which you can obtain at an office about 6 km before the Mana Pools turnoff. Make sure you don't miss the office, which is on the main road at the top of the escarpment. Before you reach that office, however, look out for the petrol filling station at Makuti, which is your last chance for a fuel stop before Mana Pools.

The untouched beauty of the place just hits you between the eyes! The Mana Pools National Park in the Zambezi Valley is Africa at its wildest.

There are some private game lodges in the region, which are open all year round and offer excellent facilities. However these are often fully booked, which means that camping is usually the order of the day. The campsites (of which 30 are available at Nyamepi) are beautifully situated on the banks of the Zambezi River, but are open in winter only, usually from May to October.

A word of warning, though. There are no fences to separate humans from the wildlife, and animals frequently visit the campsite, both by day and night. Visitors are allowed to leave the campsite unaccompanied, on foot — at their own risk. You can also rent canoes from the Park authorities, but once again, be extremely cautious. The Zambezi River is teeming with crocodile, hippo, elephant and buffalo.

My most vivid impression of Mana Pools is the canopy of trees in the area. This phenomenon is caused by foraging elephants which consume the lower branches of the trees while the higher branches are out of reach. Elephants have also kept the level of grass low and eaten many of the bushes. Visibility is therefore excellent under the leafy tree-umbrellas. Hippo are particularly prevalent in this area, especially in the Long Pool, close to Nyamepi.

Mana Pools is both a malaria and a tsetse fly area, with particularly severe infestations in the summer, and precautions are therefore essential.

Despite its rugged appearance, the park is under threat. Poachers have wreaked havoc in the area, particularly on the black rhino population; there has also been some talk about damming the Zambezi further downstream — which could have devastating consequences for the Mana Pools area.

If I may, I would like to end this section on a sad note, with a dedication to the memory of Gail Wicks (nee Decker) a beautiful young Christian lady whom we met at Mana Pools, and who was killed by a buffalo while honeymooning there. She will be sorely missed by her new husband, her family and friends … and not least by the street children of Beira, Mozambique, whom she served so lovingly.

Awesome! Inspirational! Stunning! It is impossible to find words that do justice to this scene, photographed from near the Devil's Cataract.

My wife, Margaret, clad in a hired yellow raincoat, adds scale and a touch of colour to this photograph. This picture was taken in May. Later in the year, before the summer rains and with less spray, the raincoat would have been unnecessary.

This eleven Elephant line-up was seen from Nantwich, near Robin's Camp in the west of Hwange.

At the waterhole, Nyamandhlovu, near the Main Camp in the east, Burchell's Zebra graze peacefully while *(right)* a Giraffe and her young warily approach the water.

At Nyamandhlovu, a herd of Elephant approaches the water *(main picture, opposite)*. A resident crocodile tries to stand his ground *(top and right)* but eventually, after a couple of nudges, reluctantly slides into the water *(above)*, snarling and growling — but without attempting to retaliate.

The Crowned Crane, with its distinctive comb, is unlikely to be confused with any other species. This particular bird was spotted in the veld near the Main Camp at Hwange.

At water's edge on Fothergill Island in Lake Kariba, a Buffalo chews contentedly in the company of a Cattle Egret, both blissfully unaware of their contribution to the striking white-on-black composition of the photograph.

Sunken trees at sunset near the town of Kariba.

A small group of Waterbuck, close to the Zambezi River. These beautiful antelope have a well-defined white ring around the tail, which makes them very easy to identify. They are also excellent swimmers, despite their heavy build.

(Above) Elephant are known to stand on three, and sometimes even two legs, as they stretch to reach the lower branches of the trees in the Mana Pools area. They can reach higher than a Giraffe.

(Right) In the campsite, next to our "braai" (barbecue) area, another Elephant reaches for the sky.

A Buffalo, accompanied, as usual, by Cattle Egret, grazes near the Zambezi River. On the other side of the river you can see the mountains in Zambia's Lower Zambezi National Park.

This Hippo emerged from the river, accompanied by her baby, and completely unconcerned about the foliage on her back.

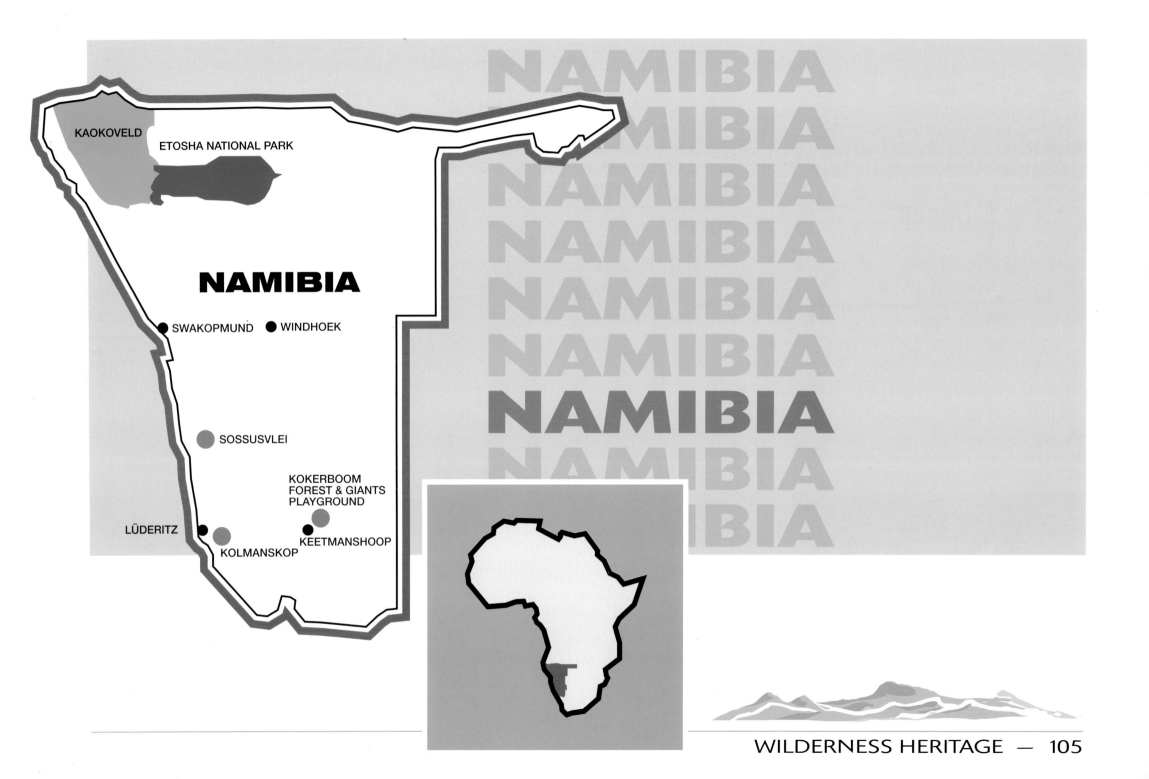

KAOKOVELD

ETOSHA NATIONAL PARK

NAMIBIA

● SWAKOPMUND   ● WINDHOEK

● SOSSUSVLEI

KOKERBOOM
FOREST & GIANTS
PLAYGROUND

LÜDERITZ

KOLMANSKOP   KEETMANSHOOP

KOLMANSKOP

No visit to the Lüderitz area is complete without a tour around Kolmanskop, which is approximately 10 km away, on the only road out of town (in the direction of Keetmanshoop).

This nostalgic ghost town dates back to before the First World War. It's a magic place, chock-full of memories of bygone times. The town (more of a village, really) consists of the eerie skeletons of diamond miners' homes, partially preserved by the dry desert air. When Kolmanskop was founded, the diamonds just lay on the surface, waiting to be discovered, and early prospectors would sprawl on their stomachs at night and pick out the sparkling gems as they glistened in the moonlight — they say a man could retrieve up to 100 carats at a time. Later, considerable digging was done, and you can still see traces of the equipment they used.

The charm of Kolmanskop lies in the ruined buildings which are decaying reminders of a gracious colonial age and of the German-speaking community which lived here in a surprising degree of comfort. In the late 1920s the prospectors were lured by richer diamond fields further south, and Kolmanskop was abandoned to the inexorably encroaching desert sand.

In its prime Kolmanskop boasted a hotel, a saloon, a bowling alley and even a casino which was the centre of entertainment, and where both local and visiting artists would perform. There was a hospital and a school, shops, a swimming pool and other amenities of town life — including a rubbish dump.

Now you will find only derelict buildings, with vacant glassless windows, invaded by the relentless desert wind and the sand ... and utter silence. But the spirit of the people who lived here somehow remains. Spend some quiet time in the houses and allow your imagination free rein. I can promise that when you leave Kolmanskop, the magic of this place and the people who once lived here will have seeped into your soul, like the sand sifting through the ruined roofs and invading rooms still decorated with faded wallpaper.

Photographically, Kolmanskop can be divided into two categories. Exterior shots of the buildings are best taken in the early morning and late afternoon, while the interiors can be photographed virtually throughout the day. There are particularly pleasing effects in the patterns of light and shade caused by the sun streaming through exposed roof timbers. Remember, though, that some of the indoor shots may entail long time exposures, and a tripod will be necessary to avoid blurring caused by camera movement.

Tours can be booked through the Kolmanskop Tour Company on telephone (09264) 6331-2445, in Lüderitz. Accommodation is available in Lüderitz at two hotels (the Bayview and Kapps Hotels) and bungalows.

There are a number of other ghost towns along the Namibian coast, including Elizabeth Bay, but at the time of writing they are not open to the public.

Palm trees in the desert? No, except in the overheated imagination of a lonely Elizabeth Bay miner in search of a wife. He advertised in a German newspaper, promising his bride-to-be that, if she joined him, she would "sleep under palm trees." This wallpaper in his desert bedroom represents his attempt to make good on that promise! (Whether the advert worked — or the bride's reaction if it did — are not on record).

KOKERBOOM FOREST AND GIANTS' PLAYGROUND

"Kokerboom" means "quiver tree", for reasons which I'll explain in a moment. However, this plant is not a tree at all, as you can gather from its botanical name *Aloe Dichotoma*.

The Kokerboom Forest (which was declared a National Monument in 1955) is situated just outside Keetmanshoop and makes an ideal stopover, with opportunities for taking excellent photographs in the late afternoon and early morning.

The kokerboom can reach heights of five to seven metres, with a trunk diameter measuring as much as one metre near the ground. It is called the "quiver tree" because in the past both Bushmen and Hottentot tribes used the longer branches to make quivers for their arrows. It invariably grows amongst black dolorite formations, which act as an anchor for the widespread but poorly developed root system. The first flowers bloom after twenty or thirty years, and the age of the plants often exceeds 300 years.

About three kilometres further along the road from Keetmanshoop you'll find the Giants' Playground, so called because the piled black rocks resemble enormous toy blocks. Kokerbooms interspersed among the rocks provide the potential for wonderful photographs of the area. If you are a really keen photographer, stay in either of these two areas after sunset to catch the afterglow — or arrive well before dawn as the first fingers of light creep into the morning sky.

One word of caution though: either follow the trail marked with arrows or take very careful note of your bearings in relation to your vehicle in the Giants' Playground. It is frighteningly easy to become confused among the rocks, and to lose all sense of where you are — especially as night falls. Accommodation is available in bungalows, with meals, showers and toilets, as well as camping facilities at the Kokerboom Forest itself. The address is:-

Mr C B Nolte
Kokerboomwoud
PO Box 262
KEETMANSHOOP
Namibia

Telephone (09264) 631-22835.

For other accommodation, there are a couple of hotels in the town of Keetmanshoop.

ETOSHA NATIONAL PARK

The Etosha National Park is situated some 500 km north of Windhoek. There are two entry points, one near Namutoni and the other near Okaukuejo. The park's main — and most famous — feature is the Etosha Pan, about 120 km from east to west, and 60 km from north to south. There are three camps in the Park: Okaukuejo on the west side, Namutoni on the eastern edge, and Halali between the two, on the southern side of the pan.

The overriding impression in Etosha is one of S-P-A-C-E … of flat vast horizons, of the

alabaster whiteness of the pan and the steel grey-blue skies. I have always found winter to be the best time for game viewing; it is the dry season and the animals are attracted to the waterholes more than in summer, when water is more freely available in the veld. The waterholes vary in origin. Some originate from artesian springs, others are known as contact springs, while some are designated as water-level springs, and others are artificially fed from boreholes.

There are more than 100 species of mammals in the Etosha National Park, and over 300 species of birdlife. It's easier to tell you which creatures are *not* found in Etosha. They are: white rhino, buffalo, hippo, crocodile and monkeys. Only the black-faced variety of impala occurs in this region.

If you are a bird lover, you will be in your element in Etosha, which is home to many rare species. Some 50 kinds of snake can be found there as well.

In the west, Okaukuejo camp has a wonderful waterhole with spotlights that are left on after dark. You'll be able to see huge herds of elephant at all hours of the day and night. Black rhino, lion, hyena, giraffe, zebra and many species of antelope (buck) are also frequent visitors to this waterhole. Photographically speaking, you will find the best viewing conditions if you walk around to the north of the waterhole (in other words, to your right) where the authorities have erected a small grandstand.

About 20 km north of Okaukuejo, on the western edge of the pan, lies the waterhole of Okondeka. Late afternoon is the best time for taking photos here. The waterhole is rather far from the parking area, but offers a wonderful view of the pan and the wide variety of animals (including lion) that visit here.

West of Okondeka is a most interesting area called the "Fairy Tale Forest", where you will be able to see the bizarre-looking moringa trees. The indigenous inhabitants called them "Upside-Down trees", and believed that they were thrown out of paradise and landed upside-down on earth.

Just to the East of Okaukuejo are the waterholes of Gemsbokvlakte, Olifantsbad and Aus, all of which are better photographically in the afternoon than in the morning. Elephant, giraffe, lion, zebra, kudu, springbok, wildebeest and gemsbok are particularly prevalent at these waterholes.

Heading eastward from Okaukuejo towards Halali, you'll come across a number of waterholes on the southern edge of the Pan, which are particularly favoured by game in the area. Homob is a good morning waterhole, although the parking area is a fair distance from the water. Then there are Sueda and Salvadora which are right on the pan. Occasionally you will be able to see cheetah and lion on the plains in the vicinity of these two waterholes.

Rietfontein, just west of Halali, is a wonderful area, with marvellous opportunities to view just about every animal in the park. Here too, the parking is a little far from the water, and you should use a long lens (just ensure that you have a steady support for the camera).

There is a recently-established waterhole at the Halali rest camp, which was opened in 1967. But because it is so new, the animals are still somewhat shy and infrequent. Just North of Halali is the parking area called Etosha. Here you travel out into the pan on a causeway for a kilometre or two. This is the only place where you can drive into the pan itself and the marvellous feeling of space is even more intense here. Relatively few animals come here — although I once saw four elephant having a glorious wallow nearby, later emerging from the white mud like four ghostly pachyderms!

East of Halali is a really good waterhole called Goas. There are two parking areas, one on the west and another on the north. I have found the north side to be better for photography, both in the morning and the afternoon. Interestingly enough, on almost every occasion that I have been to Goas, elephant have appeared from the east, spent some time at the water and then exited to the north … which is where I am invariably parked. Needless to say, I beat a hasty retreat.

As you approach Namutoni from the west, there are two excellent waterholes, Kalkheuwel and Chudob. At Kalkheuwel in particular you will be able to drive very close to the action. Huge herds of elephant and numerous other animals and birds abound in the area.

Kalkheuwel is also the only place in the park where I have spotted a Meyer's Parrot.

Just outside the Namutoni camp is the waterhole Klein Namutoni. It is excellent for afternoon photography and early morning sunrise silhouette shots.

Namutoni is a fascinating place with an interesting history. It was originally built as a fort around the turn of the century, was subsequently destroyed, then rebuilt, and eventually fell into disuse. In 1956 it was rebuilt again according to the original design, and opened as a tourist camp two years later. Visitors can stay in the fort or in mobile homes just outside. There are facilities for camping and caravanning in all the rest camps in Etosha, as well as a swimming pool at each camp.

The old fort at Namutoni on a rainy day.

North of Namutoni is Fischer's Pan, with two waterholes on its edge. One is Twee Palms and the other Aroe. Just west of Aroe, I came across a herd of elephant wallowing in a sand-bath right next to the road. When they had finished they headed toward Aroe, where we were waiting for them. I was able to take some lovely late afternoon shots of them and numerous other animals. Also close to Namutoni are the waterholes of Groot and Klein Okevi.

Just east of the Park, near Namutoni, you will find Mokuti Lodge, which is a very comfortable hotel. Game drives are organised from here on a daily basis.

I hope that this dissertation (and the practical tips) will give you the feel of Etosha and encourage you to visit the Etosha National Park. It is well worth the effort!

KAOKOVELD

Situated in northern Namibia, south of the Kunene River (which forms the border with Angola), the Kaokoveld is probably the most unspoilt area I have ever visited.

There is very little infrastructure in the area, which means that a trip to the Kaokoveld requires more planning than most holidays. A four-wheel drive vehicle is a necessity here, preferably one fitted with long-range petrol tanks. Extra space for jerry cans and containers of water is a prerequisite. And, although you might feel that there is nothing closer to nature or more romantic than sleeping under the stars, bear in mind that scorpions also sleep out — so a tent is definitely recommended!

While shooting the pictures for this section of the book, we covered 1 300 km in the Kaokoveld and carried 300 litres of fuel, 100 litres of water, and food to last us for several weeks. Our trip lasted a fortnight, over roads which varied from good to diabolical. We went in a convoy of four vehicles and the party included a medical doctor and a motor mechanic. At the very least I would recommend that you have two spare tyres with you when you go to the Kaokoveld.

One other thing … please take some plastic refuse bags with you, so that you can take out everything that you take in. Each morning we performed a can-squashing ceremony, using either two stones, or a large stone and the heel of a boot. It's worth bearing in mind that a squashed can takes up a lot less space than an unsquashed one!

The scenery in the Kaokoveld is rich and varied, ranging from the grandeur and excitement of the Epupa Falls, to the lovely valleys of the Marienfluss and Hartmann's Valley, which runs north and south right up to the Angolan border. Our most memorable adventure was traversing Van Zyl's Pass, where

it took a day and a half to cover just 27 km. It was on this occasion that our 4-wheel drive vehicle was overtaken by a man on a donkey! I have also never seen as many scorpions in one place as at the top of Van Zyl's Pass. (After some thought on the subject I decided that it was safer and easier to pitch my tent in the middle of the road). Here is where you will find the Herero-speaking Himba tribe. I first came across them near the village of Okangwati. They are a proud, statuesque people, with a culture going back several hundred years. The men and women daub their bodies from head to toe with a mixture of butterfat and ochre powder (the men add a

In the northern part of Hartmann's Valley, close to the Kunene River, the wind sometimes blows the dunes across the track. This is one of the few times that vehicles have no choice but to drive on the dunes.

darker pigment to obtain a much deeper colour than the women). The butterfat gives off quite a pungent odour, which I did not find at all unpleasant. It also acts as a protective layer against the sun and provides insulation against the cold, helping these scantily-dressed people to tolerate extremes in temperature.

The Himba are a very primitive semi-nomadic tribe, moving with their cattle and goats to where the grazing is best. As I travelled through the Kaokoveld I came across several of their villages (a fair number of which were deserted). We approached the inhabited villages carefully and respectfully, as we did not wish to disturb them or any of their traditions, especially regarding their sacred fire of mopane logs, which is kept continuously alive.

We were readily granted permission to enter their villages. The men, younger women and children were quite happy to be photographed, but the older women were distinctly camera-shy. As payment for their photographic services, the villagers asked for sweets for the children and tobacco for the adults.

Between Okangwati and the Van Zyl's Pass we stopped at a Himba burial site next to the road. The deceased must have been a chief of considerable importance, as there were at least 50 skulls of his cattle on long poles over the grave.

While I felt distinctly privileged to have been in contact with the "ochre people of the desert", there was sadness in the realisation that the influence of civilisation and access to tourists (as well as the provision of schooling) have begun to erode the traditions of the Himba, who are in danger of losing their unique cultural identity.

There is some wildlife in the Kaokoveld, which includes lion, giraffe, gemsbok (oryx), springbok, desert elephant, black rhino, ostrich, leopard and many other smaller species.

We took the route from Opuwo (on the Ruacana road) to Okangwati, and then northwards to the Epupa Falls, and finally back to Okangwati, from where we travelled westwards to Van Zyl's Pass. At the base of the pass we headed north up the Marienfluss to the Kunene River, before turning south down the Marienfluss, to Rooidrom and northwards again up Hartmann's Valley to the Angolan border. From there we drove south again — are you following all this? — skirting fairly close to the Skeleton Coast National Park. We crossed the Hoarusib and Hoanib Rivers, before travelling toward Sesfontein, and lastly southwards to Palmwag, which is in Damaraland, a very beautiful area of Namibia.

Palmwag Lodge made a welcome return to civilisation, after a couple of weeks in the Kaokoveld … especially as a restaurant, pub, and swimming pool are all part of the amenities.

One word of warning if you intend travelling in the Palmwag area (assuming of course that you have a 4x4 vehicle): it is very easy to lose your way in this part of the world. What was intended to be a 4-hour drive turned out to be an 8-hour odyssey, during which we were guided by the stars of the Southern Cross and eventually arrived back at Palmwag after 9 pm.

It was in this area that we saw the greatest number of welwitschia. These plants, which, to the eye of the uninitiated resemble an untidy sprawl of tangled stems and leaves, are sometimes more than 1000 years old, and are of interest to anyone who is even slightly botanically-minded.

At the time of writing, the Kaokoveld is not a designated National Park, so no prior booking is necessary. But it is a malaria area, so take the customary precautions (these repeated malaria warnings should not be disregarded; I know of recent cases where tourists became ill as a result of neglecting to take the medication in the prescribed dosage).

Like most of these wilderness areas, the Kaokoveld is ecologically very sensitive, and it behoves all of us to help maintain its pristine beauty by not littering, and by staying on the roads (such as they are).

SOSSUSVLEI (NAMIB DESERT)

You all know that cliché about a picture being worth more than a thousand words. Well, I have visited Sossusvlei sixteen times (as we go to press) and I can confidently say that mere words can never convey the grandeur of this compelling landscape. As a matter of fact, nor can photographs.

Sand .. silence .. solitude .. space! Sossusvlei is all this, and much, much more! The towering 400 metre orange-ochre sand dunes dwarf the camel-thorn trees at their bases. Razor-sharp ridges contrast vividly with voluptuously rounded contours, gravel plains and moonlike calcrete desert floor.

The silence hits you like an explosion ... except when the wind is blowing, or cameras are clicking! The sense of peace, of oneness with creation, of awe in the presence of nature at its most basic, pours through one's being like a primeval flood.

I can recall with especial vividness how, early one morning, a thick mist blanketed Sossusvlei. Even though I couldn't see the dunes, I could actually feel them. The trees gazed eerily at me out of the mist. I sat on a small dune, alone, and marvelled at the solitude.

I watched, fascinated, as the mist slowly lifted and unveiled a magic landscape before my eyes. It was a scene I will never forget!

(I warned you that words wouldn't do the job, but at least I'm trying).

Then there is the incredible space ... I recently climbed one of the highest dunes in Sossusvlei, and the vistas from the top were absolutely breathtaking (so, incidentally was the effort of climbing the dune). Below me stretched an ocean of sand, with every imaginable nuance of shape and texture. A lone gemsbok (oryx), king of this vast domain, crossed a nearby ridge. I stood transfixed, an insignificant speck of humanity in an infinite landscape.

I cannot wax more lyrical about it. The sheer beauty of Sossusvlei is staggering, mind-blowing, intoxicating ... and indescribable. Photographs capture only a fraction of it. The only solution is to go there and experience it yourself. But be warned: Sossusvlei is addictive!

Incidentally, I have attempted, in my modest way, to photograph this incredible area in my three previous books, *Shadows of Sand*, *Naked Wilderness* and *Introducing ... Sossusvlei* (a booklet which my wife and I produced for Sossusvlei Karos Lodge). *Shadows of Sand* depicts the pristine beauty of the place, while *Naked Wilderness* comprises female nude studies photographed in the dunes.

Sossusvlei is a sandy oasis approximately 5 km long by 5 km wide. It is roughly 70 km from the Sesriem campsite, and about 50 km from the Atlantic Ocean as the crow flies (in the interests of accuracy, I should perhaps point out that the crows generally don't fly, preferring to scavenge around the dustbins in the Sesriem campsite). The Namib, reputed to be the world's oldest desert, is only 150 km wide but about 2000 km long, stretching from southern Angola, through Namibia, to the north-west Cape in South Africa.

Wildlife tends to be restricted to gemsbok (oryx), springbok, ostrich, black-backed jackal and the Cape fox. There is also some birdlife as well as unique reptiles and insects — including the enterprising head-standing beetle which adopts a head-down posture so that the condensing dew can run down its back to the mouth. The most distinctive tree in the area is the camel-thorn tree (*Acacia Erioloba*).

Photography in the Namib Desert is both a magical experience and a daunting challenge. Without doubt the Namib (and Sossusvlei in particular) is one of the most photogenic areas in the world.

Let's talk about equipment. On the non-photographic side, a 4-wheel drive vehicle is useful, but not essential. A hat is a necessity however; so is suntan lotion and a water bottle or cold drink. Light weight walking shoes, suitable for sand, are suggested. (If you see an unusual zig-zag track in the sand, don't tread on it; you might possibly disturb a concealed Peringuey's side-winding adder, which can deliver a painful — but not fatal — bite).

Camping equipment (tents, sleeping bags, gas cookers etc.) are a must for those using the camp site at Sesriem. Just note that the gate from the outside road into the campsite opens at sunrise and closes at sunset. If you arrive after nightfall, your choices are to stay at the hotel or sleep in your car, outside the camp area. For those who prefer not to camp, the hotel in the area — the Sossusvlei Karos Lodge — has 45 rooms, is very well appointed, and is situated just outside Sesriem campsite. It really has a desert feel to it, with the emphasis on ecological correctness and a Bedouin-tent appearance, in all the earthy tones of the surrounding desert. Bookings can be made through their Central Reservations Office in Johannesburg.

If you want to travel down to the far end of Sossusvlei, you'll need a four-wheel drive vehicle for the last 5 km — you can now rent a suitable vehicle from The Sossusvlei 4x4 Rental which operates from the hotel. This company can also meet you at the Sesriem runway if you are flying in from Windhoek for the day. Whatever your mode of transport, please don't leave the designated roads in your vehicle. By doing so you are not only spoiling other peoples' photographs (tyre tracks can stay visible for a long time — even decades — after you have left) but you will be disturbing the very fragile ecology.

Another recent development is the introduction of a balloon trip over the desert with Namib Sky Adventure Safaris. They operate from Camp Mwisho which is situated about 50 km south of Sesriem on the road to Lüderitz. It is an unforgettable experience to drift silently over the Namib in the early morning, looking down on an ocean of sand with its endless vista of shadow and light. An elegant champagne breakfast — complete with chairs, tables and linen — awaits you at a landing spot in the middle of nowhere. For more information phone (09264) 6632 and ask for 5703.

Sesriem camp is administered by the Department of Agriculture and Nature Conservation, Private Bag 13267, Windhoek, Namibia. Their telephone number is (09264) 61-236975. Incidentally there is now a swimming pool in the camp and cold drinks, beers, postcards and books are on sale at the office. Drinking water is also available, as well as an ablution block with toilets, showers and hot and cold water.

The ghost town of Kolmanskop, near Lüderitz, has been standing for nearly a century. These ruined remains are a stark reminder of the town's long-departed inhabitants, their way of life, their joys, their sorrows. It is indeed a reminder of the fleeting nature of life itself.

Doorways to the past … sand-filled rooms where comfortable furniture once stood … peeling walls with wallpaper ghosts … decaying skeletons that were once called home.

Once a beautiful mansion … now home to the sand,
the stars, and the silence.

A Kokerboom (Quiver Tree) among the sun-blackened rocks of the Kokerboom Forest.

Sunrises and sunsets in the Kokerboom Forest are spectacular and memorable. *(On a technical note, the tree on the opposite page was lit with a flashgun, while the setting sun illuminated the distant clouds — a technique known as "synchro-sun").*

Moonrise over the Kokerboom Forest, with the afterglow of the departed sun lingering on the trunks of the trees.

The bizarre balancing rocks of the Giants' Playground offer tremendous photographic opportunities for those with a free and vivid imagination.

(Left) Storm clouds gather on the road between the Kokerboom Forest and the Fish River Canyon.

(Above) The Okondeka waterhole, just north of Okaukuejo. Looking east, the Etosha Pan stretches 120 km from this point.

(Opposite page, bottom) A herd of wildebeest trek along the edge of the Pan, heading for a waterhole.

(Opposite page, top left) A Gemsbok (Oryx) stands close to the Pan, which has filled with water at the end of the rainy season in April. (Compare this picture with the photograph on the previous page).

(Opposite page, top right) A Black Rhino walks through the veld near Okaukuejo.

(This page) The Moringa trees, or "Upside-down trees" in the "Fairy Tale Forest" north-west of Okaukuejo. I am sure you'll agree with me that the branches look like inverted roots.

(*Opposite*) Two Elephants prepare to do battle at the Okaukuejo waterhole, among the white stones which are so typical of Etosha.

(*This page, top*) Enjoying a sand-bath near the Aroe waterhole, north of Fischer's Pan and Namutoni.

(*Inset*) A baby Elephant chasing birds at the Goas waterhole, near Halali.

The Predators

(Top left) A juvenile Spotted Hyena extracts a thorn from its foot. Hyenas are very efficient hunters and scavengers, and are said to possess the strongest set of jaws of any predator in Africa.

(Top right) A pair of Black-backed Jackals socialising before commencing the hunting and scavenging business of the day.

(Left) A majestic African Lion at the Gemsbokvlakte waterhole near Okaukuejo.

The Prey

(Top left) A herd of Zebra slaking their thirst. Because there were Lion in the area, they were extremely nervous and I had no more than a couple of seconds to take this photograph.

(Top right) A magnificent male Kudu, its horns glinting in the sun, stays close to its mate.

(Right) The Black-faced Impala. According to some estimates, there are not more than 1000 of this endangered species left. They are found in Etosha, Damaraland and the Southern Kaokoveld. The main feature which distinguishes them from the more common Impala is the black flash down the nose.

129

(Above) I had to wait for the sun to drop into the right position — while hoping that the Giraffe wouldn't change direction. I was lucky!
(Opposite page) Two kilometres outside the Namutoni Camp (and knowing I had to be in camp by sunset) I shot this photograph with a 600 mm lens and 2x converter (1/2000 second at ƒ11) and nearly blinded myself in the process. My suggested title is *Giraffic Park*.

The silhouette of a large Baobab tree on the Southern bank of the Kunene River, near the Epupa Falls.

Early morning photographs of the Epupa Falls. The campsite is about 100 metres from the Falls.

(Above and top right) Two Himba men, their wizened features etched with character and the wisdom of many years, reflect on the past. *(Right)* Five Himba children act as herdboys to their parents' Nguni cattle.

(Far left) A beautiful Himba maiden shows off her ochre-coloured headgear and necklaces.

(Left) My Nissan Sani 4x4 eases down a steep slope on the Van Zyl's Pass. The camera wasn't tilted to exaggerate the steep slope — as you can see from the vertical trees on either side of the vehicle!

(Below) A Himba man on his donkey overtakes our convoy with four-footed ease on Van Zyl's Pass.

The photographs on these two pages convey something of the seemingly endless space that is so typical of the Kaokoveld — attributable, in part, to the absence of fences. You also see two of the smaller fry that we encountered in the Marienfluss.

(Left) On the Western side of Hartmann's Valley, with the dunes of the Skeleton Coast in the background, a Welwitschia Mirabilis plant sprawls across the ground. Each plant possesses only two leaves, and its roots extend no more than three metres below the ground. The Welwitschia is a dioeceous species, which means that the male and female plants are completely separate.

(Main picture, right) A herd of Gemsbok (Oryx) feeding on the plain, are dwarfed by enormous mountains in the South-Western part of the Kaokoveld.

(Right) The Nara Melon is another of the Namib's most characteristic plants. Its long roots reach down to water far below the surface. Nara Melon seeds have been found in archaeological diggings, and were obviously important to early man.

(Top left and left) Some of the Giraffe we encountered as we headed eastwards along the Hoanib River towards Sesfontein. It seemed quite odd to find these animals in such an arid region.

(Above) Incredibly thick sand forced us to use low-range 4x4 engaged in second gear. (A tip: In thick sand, choose a low gear and stay in it! To lose traction by changing gear, even for a second, would be disastrous. It is in this area, West of Sesfontein, among the Mopane trees, that the desert Elephant is often encountered.

(This page and overleaf) An Herero village near Sesfontein braces itself for a drenching as the heavens open.

Red dawn in the Namib. No colour filters were used in this photograph, or any others in this book. As an example of the astonishing variety of the Sossusvlei landscape, this photograph and those on the next six pages were all taken from the same spot.

In the light of dawn, with the sun caressing the sensuous curves of the sand, the similarity between dunes and nudes becomes inescapable.

This large dune *(left)* took me several hours to climb in pre-dawn darkness, and only a few minutes to slide down. *(Right)* Looking over the 2x4 parking area, this early morning photograph picks up the pastel shades on the dunes, while the valley is still largely in shadow.

TIPS ON DESERT PHOTOGRAPHY

Do not leave a camera body lying around without a lens attached to it. With two camera bodies available, I try never to change lenses in the desert, for fear of sand getting in and fouling up the works.

Never leave your camera equipment lying in the sun. It will damage both equipment and film. (Even inside the camera, film can be harmed by excessive heat).

Have your equipment ready at all times, especially your long lens. When photographing from the car, I ask my passenger to sit in the back, so that I can have my equipment in front and shoot through both windows (open, of course). With this arrangement I can focus and shoot within about 5 seconds of coming to a standstill. So incidentally can my passenger in the back.

Take more film than you think you're likely to need.

If your hair is a little thin on top (refer to author's picture on the back of the book jacket), wear a soft-brimmed hat rather than a peaked cap, which tends to get in the way of the viewfinder.

Carry essential rations (like water and a snack) with you whenever you leave your car.

I find that April, May and June are excellent months to photograph the Namib. Other months can be good as well, but these three are usually not too hot, not too cold, and not too windy.

If you are photographing the large shadowed surface of a dune, with only limited sunny areas, override your camera's automatic system and underexpose (otherwise the built-in light meter will try to render the dark areas as mid-grey and in so doing will over-expose the bright areas).

The converse is also true. Large areas of white clay, for instance, should be over-exposed, otherwise your photographs will turn out a dull grey.

If you are shooting with a wideangle lens and want to emphasise the ripples in the sand as a lead-in, while still maintaining focus on the horizon, don't hesitate to switch the camera to aperture priority and shoot at f22, even if that means using a slow shutter speed of around 1/8 second (this is where your tripod will come into its own.) That way you will ensure maximum depth of field and sharpness.

Go to Sossusvlei with an open mind, as far as composition is concerned. Remember — your imagination is your only limitation.

Allow a minimum of three or four days, to give your eye time to adjust to the compositional possibilities of the dunes. For the most effective pictures, I have found a 100–300 mm lens to be the best.

Don't dash around all over the place in your vehicle during good lighting time, which ends two hours after dawn and starts again two hours before sunset. Take all the pictures you can in a particular area, then move on. During the rest of the day, scout around for new areas to photograph, so that you can be ready for the next period of favourable light.

(Left) Taking off at dawn from Camp Mwisho, about 50 km South of Sesriem.

(Above) A magical experience, drifting over the Namib in a hot-air balloon.

(Far left) An aerial view of a galloping Gemsbok (Oryx).

(Top left) Sossusvlei Karos Lodge, just outside Sesriem camp.

(Right) Although Sossusvlei is only 60 km from the coast, misty scenes like this are unusual … I have encountered mist in Sossusvlei only twice in seventeen trips.

(Facing page, left) Another aerial view, looking toward the Naukluft Mountains to the east of the Namib Desert.

(Left) Ripples in the sand echo the pattern of "herring-bone" clouds, with a dead Camelthorn tree as a focal point.

Single Gemsbok (Oryx) can often be seen on the road between Sesriem and Sossusvlei. Once in a while, however, I have come across a whole herd — which, on one memorable occasion, numbered more than fifty animals.

Gemsbok have an amazing ability to withstand searing heat. In summer, when ground temperatures can soar up to 60 °C, the Gemsbok copes by means of a natural heat-exchanger system in its moist nasal passages, which helps to maintain a constant body temperature.

(Above): Backlit grass provides the focal point for this photograph — as well as a source of food and moisture in this arid environment.

(Opposite page) A huge 400 m high sand dune dwarfs a couple of camel-thorn trees *(Acacia Erioloba)*, near Dune 45.

160

Dawn near Dune 45. Because the large dune in the background is in deep shadow, correct exposure can only be achieved by underexposing the film ½ to 1 stop.

The photographs on this and the next few pages were all taken in the Dead Vlei. About 4 km along the 4x4 track, there is now a specific parking area for the Dead Vlei. About 20 minutes' walk in a southerly direction, over a couple of small dunes, will bring you to what I consider to be the quietest place on earth.

A corner of the Dead Vlei at sunset.

It has been suggested that the Dead Vlei was once covered by sand. This helped preserve these trees, which could easily be 500 years old.

While most of the trees in the Dead Vlei have died, there are one or two which are still alive.